# the outdoor kitchen

**LIVE-FIRE COOKING FROM THE GRILL**

Eric Werner of Hartwood
with Nils Bernstein

Photography by Gentl and Hyers
Illustrations by Emily Isabella

TEN SPEED PRESS
California | New York

To Mya: my partner, friend, and the love of my life.

Through your confidence, strength, and creativity,
I am forever inspired.

# Contents

# Foreword

I have always been attracted to fire. As a kid, playing with fire was always taboo, and being a kid who always got into trouble, it was my go-to for mischief. Fire seemed uncontrollable, destructive, and angry, and I could connect to all of that. At first, it was an empty field, then a patch of woods, then an abandoned house. Of course, when the authorities got involved, I had to stop. I was a pyromaniac in the making, but I had no idea it would later become a talent and not a curse.

When I started cooking in 1980, no one was using anything but gas, and the fire was intense, but it wasn't enough. When I went to Puglia on a sabbatical, I found a place where cooking with big wood-burning ovens was the norm. Large caves filled with smoke and burning logs were adding another dimension to simple food. Terra-cotta bowls filled with creatures of the sea were coming out charred and sweet and delicious. Fire was calling my name again, but this time it was summoning me to create, not destroy. When I returned to New York City in 1990, I opened my first kitchen with a wood-burning oven, and I continue to cook with fire to this day.

Cooking with fire is not easy. This primitive technique has a lot of nuances that need to be learned. You cannot rush fire. You need to listen to it, learn where the hot spots are, and look at the coals or wood to figure out the timing. There is no gauge, no thermometer—it takes intuition. Only someone looking for the hard way will be attracted to it, someone fearless, someone like Eric Werner.

The first time I met Eric was in 2000. My team and I had just opened Peasant, and this skinny kid with a big grin and tattoos down his arm was in the kitchen asking to speak with me. He told me he loved my restaurant and that he was a young cook fresh out of culinary school. He shared that he had a space on Clinton Street with a wood-burning oven and asked whether I would go over and take a look at it. Of course, I had absolutely no time, but he and I had some mutual friends, and I was curious; there was something about this kid that made me want to check out his space. When I finally got there, I found it was a hole, but it had an immense wood-burning oven. Eric had some crazy ideas about what he was going to do, and he seemed a little naive but mostly rebellious and determined. I somehow recognized that Eric was a lot like myself and that he would make it work, no matter what.

When Eric got together with Mya, I thought that now he had an anchor to keep his dreams from flying away and that she would ground him. But I was wrong. When these two kids told me about opening a restaurant in Tulum, I thought, okay. Then they told me about a jungle plot that was across the street from the beach, and I thought, wow. When they told me there was no roof, no electricity, no running water, I thought, what??? This kid has finally surpassed me in the crazy department, and his windmill is an oven in the middle of a swampy jungle and his lance a shovel and a strong back. Eric and Mya's vision of Hartwood came alive by sheer faith and determination and heart. The first time I tasted Eric's food was sitting at a table in that jungle, smelling the wood fire burning, mixed with citrus and fresh flavors all around, and watching the flames dance around Eric's head. He was smiling that big grin again, and I was jealous and very, very proud.

**Frank DeCarlo**

# Part One

# The Outdoor Kitchen

# Introduction

All of my earliest memories of cooking are over open fire. My mother died when I was very young and my dad and I moved around a lot from country town to country town in upstate New York. My dad worked construction and was a real outdoorsman, so there wasn't a lot of cooking going on in the house. He would hunt venison after work during the week, and we'd cut it up in the backyard, cook it on the grill, and that was dinner. Maybe we'd boil some corn with it. We also ate at a lot of roadside grills, those public grilling areas off the side of the road in the mountains. In the winter, we'd go ice fishing and people would have grills on the ice. So there wasn't a lot of salad making, but it created an association in me of food with fire, nature, and family—something that brings people together.

My father passed away when I was twelve, and I was sent to boarding school in the Catskills. They had a kitchen with a large grill on the side of a mountain next to a lake. That was where I spent most of my time. It was almost like a trade school, teaching the basics of how to cook, with most of our meals made over open fire. Eventually I was in charge of the meals for about seventy-five kids for breakfast, lunch, and dinner. I started seeing cooking as something I could focus on to make a living. My guidance counselor recommended that I go to culinary school, and the most esteemed one in the country—the Culinary Institute of America (CIA)—was only ninety minutes away in New York.

I studied at CIA, but I left after the first year and a half because I couldn't afford it anymore, and I was bursting at the seams to be part of a real professional kitchen. My first job was as a pastry chef at Payard in New York City. I worked for free—it felt like a better way to get an education and had better potential for making connections than being at school—and when I finished my 1:00 a.m. to 11:00 a.m. shift, I'd work at a deli from noon to 7:00 p.m. to make money.

My next job was working at 71 Clinton Fresh Food Group with Wylie Dufresne, who was a big proponent of molecular gastronomy. But in my mind, I wanted to get back to cooking over fire, which I was able to do for several years at Peasant with Frankie DeCarlo and Dulci DeCarlo. That's where I really started to understand the different ways that cooking over wood fire could elevate food, as well as the joy it brought the cooks and the diners. Peasant was the best education I could possibly have had, but after six years there, I really wanted to make American farm-to-table food (Peasant was Italian, specifically Puglia). I went to work at Vinegar Hill House in Brooklyn and was working there when my soon-to-be-wife, Mya, and I took a vacation to Tulum, Mexico.

As a restaurant worker, I was always working and always broke, so I'd never really taken a vacation, let alone to Mexico. I knew nothing about Tulum, but it felt raw and exciting. Mya is very brave, and we wanted an adventure, so we returned a few times more, talking each visit about the possibility of living and working there. I knew I wanted to cook over open fire and to do something sensitive to the place and its people and resources. I had tons of restaurant experience by the time we decided to pull the trigger on opening Hartwood in a remote corner of Tulum, but nothing could prepare me for this last decade of living and cooking in the Yucatán jungle.

Outside of Argentina or Uruguay, there's no better country than Mexico in which to get an education in open-fire cooking. There are so many ingenious grill designs that are fascinating and inexpensive and get the job done beautifully. Almost any large neighborhood market will have simple standing *anafres*, steel braziers with ash pans underneath, over which you place a *comal* (griddle) or grill grates. These are common in backyards and among street vendors. For larger capacity, *tambos*—steel drum barrels—are commonly sawed in half to make two large receptacles for wood fire. I've seen steel-mesh chairs and even shopping carts set over in-ground fire pits. If you think that great grilling involves a lot of store-bought equipment and a capacious backyard, your mind will quickly change when you see a group of people making carne asada on the wheel cap of a car tire over a fire built on the side of the road.

Mya and I moved to Tulum in 2010 and opened Hartwood, a restaurant located at the edge of town, between the ocean and the jungle. We now split our time between there and our family home in the Catskills. When we're in Tulum, I'm always at the restaurant, so I really look forward to my free time in the Catskills, where I can relax at the grill with Mya and our daughter, Charlie. My love for the mountains has never left me. I love the change of seasons, and how the ingredients—and the feeling of cooking outside—are so different from month to month. Grilling isn't something I do only when it's sunny out; if anything, I prefer being around a hot grill when it's cold. The smell and taste of wood-grilled food has a coziness that's perfectly suited to fall and winter, though I love working with the vegetables, fruits, and herbs of spring and summer.

Cooking outdoors over live fire defines what cooking is for me. It's simple, it's tactile, it's foolproof, and most of all, it brings out the best flavors. No two fires are ever the same, which means your food will never turn out the same way—

and that's a good thing. It's not about precise cooking times and temperatures but simply paying attention. You don't have to obsess over perfection, which makes it relaxing and inspiring in ways that other methods of cooking aren't.

This book translates how I cook at Hartwood to American backyards. Hartwood isn't a Mexican restaurant; it has always been a marriage of my American training with Mexican ingredients. There are so many ingredients native to Mexico—corn, tomatoes, squash, beans—that define American cooking as well (much of the United States used to be Mexico, after all). Even things like fresh and dried chiles, pumpkin seeds, and tomatillos are becoming part of the American larder and can be found in any large supermarket. So I hope this book represents a modern vision of American outdoor cooking.

The grill described and photographed throughout this book is the exact one I use at home, which is a smaller replica of what I use at Hartwood. It has all but replaced our indoor kitchen. It's not just for grilling meat: anything cooked on a stovetop—and in some cases, an oven—can be done in my outdoor kitchen. Hopefully, this book will broaden what outdoor cooking means to you. Rather than obsessing over the technical aspects of grilling, I just want you to cook outside and see what happens.

# My Outdoor Kitchen

My grill design is very basic, but it took years to perfect. Since there is no gas or electricity at Hartwood, we have to cook every part of every dish with wood fire. The first Hartwood grill was stone based, but the constant high heat was destroying it. Adding iron helped with performance, but warping was a problem. It really wasn't until our fifth year that we ended up with the kitchen we use today and the one that I'm going to teach you to build in the following pages. There are so many small considerations, and there was a lot of trial and error to get to this point.

At Hartwood, the grill is carrying a very high burn load for fourteen hours a day, every day, and then it sits outside in the cold at night. When metal constantly alternates between hot and cold, it can warp like crazy. It took adjusting both the thickness and the shape of the iron to eliminate the warping issues. Maintenance is simple—you just wipe it out and oil it down—but if it's not done, the grill can get rusted out, or the metal can start chipping. The shape was really hard to get right as well. If there is too much distance between the top and base of the grill, you have to burn too much wood; if it's too low, you can't get enough of an ember bed to generate sufficient heat. We also had problems with airflow and air direction, which play a major part. The front is open, but there's also a small amount of air intake on the back of the grill. You want enough oxygen intake to fuel the fire, without letting in so much that the coals die out too fast and smolder. Even the sizing of the grill grates is important, not just for attractive grill marks but to carry enough heat at the surface. The whole contraption works like a seasoned cast-iron pan; even if you were to remove all the coals, it would stay hot for at least an hour. And its shape and size make it just as easy to light up a few logs on one side to grill a rib eye for one as it is to cook dinner for thirty friends.

The grill design in this book really is an outdoor kitchen, in that any cooking method can be done on it. Of course, you will use it for grilling, for the unmistakable flavor that comes from wood fire licking the food directly, but anything you do on a stovetop can also be done here—sautéing, boiling, deep-frying, steaming—without being limited to 8-inch-diameter burners and standardized Btus. You can also cook more aggressively, confidently charring your food, knowing that the smoke will fade into the sky rather than into the walls of your house. At the restaurant, I added a wood-fired oven, smoker, and rotisserie, but these are things you can do over time if you like. I hope you'll take the effort to make my outdoor kitchen. It's a fun, fast, and beautiful way to cook that provides an immense sense of satisfaction. The grill is an heirloom that gets better with use and will last several lifetimes.

# Fire and Iron

Almost everyone in the United States is grilling on a gas grill or a charcoal grill made of thin stainless steel or aluminum. These can make delicious food, but to me, they're a missed opportunity on many levels.

Gas grills don't get hot enough to properly sear, char, and create dark grill marks and crusts that lock in flavor and juices. They max out at a much lower temperature than a wood-fired grill. You also get no flavor from the heat source itself, as you do from wood and (to a lesser degree) charcoal. The grill box is hard to clean, and it can be a hassle to keep refilling the propane tank. In most cases, for the recipes in this book, I'd recommend cooking on a cast-iron pan over a high flame in your kitchen rather than cooking on a gas grill.

Charcoal grills, like the ubiquitous Weber kettle-style grills, are a great introduction to grilling. But use hardwood in them. Learn how to light and manage a wood fire and watch how it turns into embers. Build the embers higher or lower to see how that affects the surface heat. Tuck some veggies in the embers and cook something in a cast-iron pan set on the embers. Since firewood is all-natural (as opposed to charcoal briquettes), you don't have to worry about food coming in contact with it. And if your kettle grill doesn't have cast-iron grill grates, you can buy those separately online.

At the end of the day, though, you're cooking on thin painted aluminum or stainless steel that has nowhere near the heat capacity of a thick iron grill body. Iron not only retains heat well but it also radiates heat far better than thin stainless steel or aluminum. Holding your hand just above the surface of a hot aluminum or stainless steel pan is much easier than with a cast-iron pan (this is why, for example, potatoes roasted in a cast-iron pan crisp up better than those cooked on a baking sheet). It takes a lot of wood to keep these going, while a small amount of wood in an iron grill can create an environment that stays extremely hot for a long time. There's also no access to the wood while cooking, making it almost impossible to adjust the heat when the grill grates are on. This is all-important when you're cooking multiple things on the grill.

If you don't already have an outdoor grill, or even if you do, you can also buy a cast-iron hibachi-style grill. (Lodge makes a good one.) Though they don't have much surface area, this will bring you closer to the type of grilling that my outdoor kitchen does. You may be limited by how much you can cook simultaneously and by how easily you can manage the embers, but hopefully you'll get comfortable building and managing wood fire.

Most importantly, these grills are boring. They don't create a conversation, they don't invite people to crowd around, and they don't encourage everyone to play with the food. Your food takes longer to cook and doesn't taste as good. And your grill is no different from any of the millions that were bought at a generic home-improvement store. Do you want a mass-produced product or an heirloom that is handmade, indestructible, and beautiful?

### Hacking Your Weber

There are two things you can do to grill better using your existing Weber or other charcoal-style grill. The best is to have a custom iron grill grate made. Bring your existing grate to an ironworker to use as a template. Have handles added, since it will be extremely heavy. This will also start your relationship with the ironworker, which will hopefully lead to having your own outdoor kitchen built. The second is to always use hardwood. This will allow you to cook directly on or in the embers as well as learn how to manage the fire and create varying heat levels.

# How to Build Your Own Outdoor Kitchen

I refer to my grill as cast iron, since it looks and acts like it. Technically, though, it's mild steel, a type of carbon steel which actually has a higher percentage of iron than cast iron (cast iron is iron with over 2 percent carbon; carbon steel is iron with less than 2 percent carbon). Cast iron must be poured into molds and is quite brittle, which is partly why cast-iron cookware is so thick. Mild steel is more malleable and also has a smoother texture than cast iron, helping prevent sticking, especially as you build up a seasoning (carbon steel seasons in the same way as cast iron).

These details and illustrations are what you should bring your ironworker, but they can be tweaked and personalized in any ways that you and your ironworker agree on. This is what works for my family, but, for example, you can make the overall footprint smaller or larger, or a different shape altogether. The most important thing is the height of the firebox and the heft of the grill grates and firebox.

I can't stress enough how satisfying it is to have this grill made. Besides the joy of cooking on it, the process of designing and building it with the ironworker is enjoyable and the result is a one-of-a-kind outdoor kitchen that will last for generations.

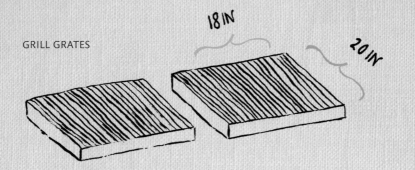

GRILL GRATES

18 IN

20 IN

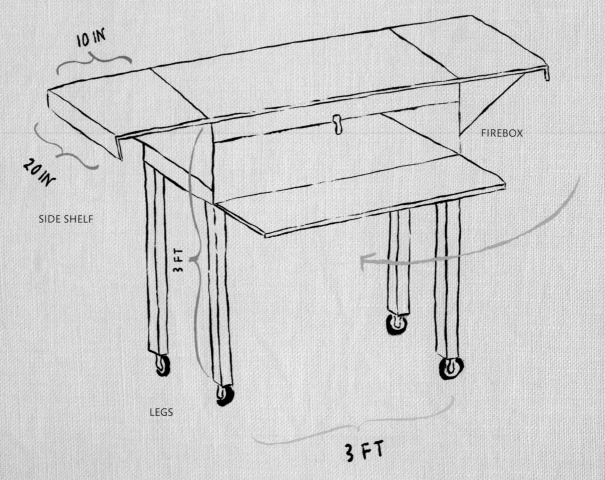

10 IN

20 IN

SIDE SHELF

LEGS

3 FT

SIDE SHELF

FIREBOX

3 FT

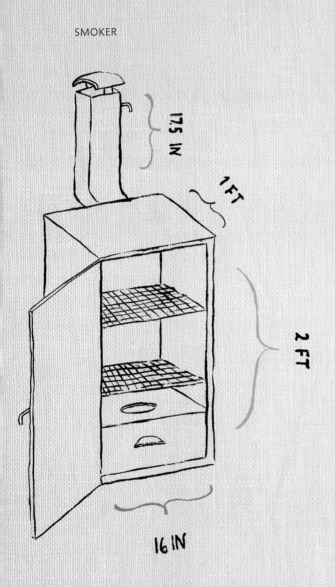

SMOKER

17.5 IN

1 FT

2 FT

16 IN

# Building the Grill

### Firebox

The firebox, made of $^3/_{16}$-inch-thick mild steel, is 36 inches long, 8 inches high, and 20 inches deep. There are 3 small rectangular openings cut into the back of it for oxygen intake; each opening measures about 3 inches long by 2 inches high, spaced evenly. There is a hinged door that stays shut with a latch. I almost always cook with mine open, but closing it can help lower the temperature by limiting oxygen intake, and protecting your fire from strong winds .

### Grill Grates

Because the grill grates are thick and heavy, it's best to have two (each measuring 18 inches by 20 inches) rather than one large one. Each individual grate is about $^1/_8$-inch thick and $^1/_2$-inch deep, with $^3/_4$- to 1-inch spacing between each one. You want that depth so the grates retain and emit more heat than if they were made of thin rods or sheet metal with holes cut into them. The grates should drop into $^1/_2$-inch-angle iron on the inside perimeter of the grill, so the tops are level with the top of the firebox.

### Legs

The legs are made from 2 by 2 by $^1/_4$-inch square tube steel. Add locking casters so the grill can be easily moved.

### Side Shelves

The shelves aren't technically necessary, but you will be happy you added them, giving yourself adequate space to work without having to leave the grill. Think of it as a kitchen countertop. I find it handy to have these shelves to keep my tongs, rags, oil, and other tools, and my food just before or after it's on the grill. Since these shelves don't need to retain heat, you can use thin steel; 10 by 20 inches is a good size. The shelves can be removable, or

connected with handcrafted high-heat hinges. Hinged rods made of ³⁄₈-inch-round bar hold the shelves up when in use.

## Building the Smoker

The smoker, made of ³⁄₁₆-inch-thick mild steel, is an entirely separate piece, not connected in any way to the grill. However, have the ironworker size the smoker height so that it can slide under the grill, with the flue coming out the back (the flue is also called the exhaust damper and is what allows gases to escape). Mine is about 24 inches high, 16 inches wide, and 12 inches deep.

There's an 8-inch box with a drawer at the base of the smoker where you put the embers for smoking. There should be a 4-inch-diameter hole at the top of the box and another one at the back that has some sort of latched or sliding door that allows you

to open or close it. Be sure this door fits well and allows virtually no air to escape. This is the intake damper, which allows oxygen to keep the embers hot. Partially closing the intake damper helps reduce the heat in the smoker; fully close the intake damper and the flue extinguishes the embers. Add a knob or latch to the front of the box so you can easily open it to add embers.

The flue is made of 3-inch flue pipe, with an intake damper that can open and close. I like having two shelves in the smoker to smoke multiple things at once; the shelves are also a convenient place to hold food before serving. These shelves are made of heavy-duty expanded metal, sitting on a 1¼ by 1¼ by ³⁄₁₆-inch angle on three sides (the left, right, and back). Finally, the entire smoker should have a hinged door so that the smoke is fully contained.

## Finishing the Grill and the Smoker

Have your ironworker paint every exterior surface of the grill and smoker (except the grates) with an industrial-grade heat- and rust-resistant paint. These come in many colors for easy personalization of your grill. Buy long, sturdy S-hooks to place along the back of the grill to hang pots and pans.

## Smoking

If you're having the grill made, you may as well build a smoker at the same time. Since it fits under the grill, it doesn't take up any additional space. Besides having smoking at your disposal any time you grill, it's also a handy place to keep cooked food warm, to stash food in case of a sudden rainstorm, or to store embers when you want to reduce the heat on the grill.

Smoking is just a matter of adding more or fewer embers to the smoker box to maintain temperature. Get an instant-read oven thermometer and let it sit on, or hang from, one of the shelves indefinitely. You want the heat to register between 220° and 240°F for raw meat, though it can be a little lower for cooked meat, seafood, vegetables, and fruit.

If you choose not to build the smoker, it's still easy to infuse wood smoke into food that doesn't need to be cooked through (including meat and seafood that have already been cooked on the grill). With an all-wood fire, you're already making tasty smoke. You can just put embers in a stockpot or on a sheet pan, put the food near them without touching (in a heatproof dish or on layers of aluminum foil), and cover everything tightly with foil for at least 30 minutes. It will create a very hot environment at first, but the lack of oxygen will extinguish the embers, gradually cooling the pot or sheet pan down while retaining the smoke.

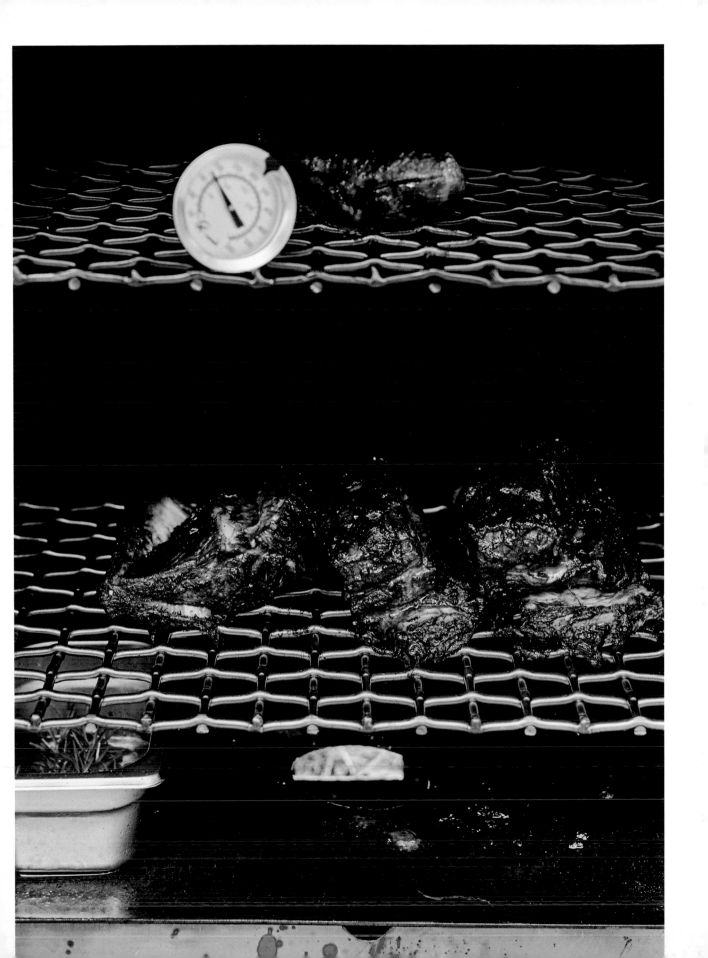

# Piotr the Ironworker

"Polish are accepted. Everybody else gets turned into sausage."

That's the welcome sign at P&M Welding in Pine Island, New York. I'm not Polish, but I think I was spared the meat grinder because building my outdoor kitchen is the type of job that most ironworkers love. It's the best kind of DIY project because . . . you don't do it yourself. No matter your skill level or interest in welding, this project is something best left to an actual ironworker. And yet the process of working with that person is really satisfying in its own right. You keep an old craft and a local business alive—supporting your community, not a corporation. I guarantee there is one (if not dozens) in your immediate area that would be happy to build this (just google "metal fabrication," "welding," or "ironworker").

It took maybe five minutes to get the grill project rolling with Piotr. I called him up and said, "Would you be able to make a grill for cooking?" and he replied, "If it's made of iron, of course." I drove over and gave him my design and the dimensions, just sketched out on a piece of paper, even a simpler version than the blueprint in this book. He said, "No problem. I'll give you a price in three days."

I got the grill in about three weeks. Even though I was the one who had designed this thing, during those three weeks, I felt like a little kid waiting for Christmas. I never had that feeling bringing something back from a store or waiting for a delivery person.

It's a fun project for both the ironworker and the grill owner. Piotr seemed as if he was enjoying it because I'm sure he doesn't get a lot of grills to build, and I felt as if I was helping to create something exciting for my family. I kept my grill pretty straightforward, but there are any number of ways you can customize it. The outside is coated in a high-temperature outdoor paint, available in an array of colors. You can weld any pattern onto it, or even add your initials, your grandmother's ladle, or devil horns. Grilling is about connecting and bringing people together in ways that other cooking methods don't. Building this grill creates a connection before you even make your first meal.

# Buying Wood

Some people get really into wood, assessing how different hardwoods contribute different tastes, how differently they burn, the environmental issues around each one, and their own nostalgic connections to the wood. There's a lot of info out there about hardwoods, and I encourage you to learn about them. But ultimately, all you really need to do is buy seasoned firewood and light it. It's no different from lighting charcoal briquettes and in fact is usually easier.

You can buy small quantities of seasoned hardwood at most larger hardware stores, supermarkets, or online; this is a good way to start. This wood will be correctly labeled and free of insects. It's also kiln-dried and lights very quickly. When you're ready to commit to a larger and more economical quantity (and have the room to store it), buy a cord of wood from a local dealer. A cord measures 4 feet high by 4 feet deep by 8 feet wide. Some dealers sell "face cords," which are only the depth of an individual log (under 2 feet); keep this in mind when comparing prices.

Do some research in your area to find a firewood seller with high recommendations. A simple google search for "firewood," and your city should bring up many options, so ratings and recommendations are key. Some unscrupulous dealers mix in softwood or stack the wood in such a way that you get less than promised. A reputable seller will sell only properly seasoned (that is, dried for at least six months) hardwood in the promised quantity and free of extreme insect infestation. You should cook only with hardwood—such as oak, beech, alder, hickory, walnut, pecan, maple, mesquite, and fruitwoods—because softwoods such as pine, cedar, fir, and spruce create a bitter, resinous smoke.

Keep your firewood outside, covered with a tarp. The fresh air helps to keep it dry, and wood can harbor insects that you don't want inside your house. I keep my wood close to the grill. Firewood can stay outside like this year-round, no matter your climate.

## Lump Charcoal

Lump charcoal is charcoal made entirely from hardwood, with none of the fillers of charcoal briquettes. Lump charcoal burns fast, hot, and evenly, with good flavor. Still, I always prefer cooking with wood, because I like the mix of the embers' even heat with the licking flames and the smoke from burning wood. Any of your embers that don't turn to ash are lump charcoal, and you can mix them into your next fire.

## When the Grill Arrives

Place the grill at least 10 feet from anything flammable such as bushes and trees, as well as your house. Before cooking on the grill for the first time, build a good-size fire to burn off any residue from the construction process. Let the fire die out on its own (once there are no more flames, you can stop monitoring it), then clean out the wood and ash, and rub the whole thing with a thin natural oil (like vegetable oil). Just oil a rag and rub down every exposed area, including the grill grates, joints, corners, and so on. This will help prevent rust and chipping. Now you're good to go.

You don't need any special cover besides a tarp. Look for any waterproof tarp that's at least 10 by 12 feet. I use one that I bought online, and I leave it outside year-round. If you don't cover your grill and it gets wet, just tilt the water out of it and let it dry in the sun. If you do get a little rust, cover the rusted area with a paste of salt and vinegar for 10 minutes, then scrub with a wire brush. It's a good habit to oil the grill after you clean it out, but you really only need to do that every five or so uses. You do want to oil the grill grates before adding food, just to discourage sticking. Over time, the high temperatures will polymerize the fat and give you an essentially nonstick surface.

## Starting and Managing Your Fire

A bag of wood should come with a plastic bag of kindling, but any piece of pine will work as a firestarter, as will a wooden paint stirrer, disposable wooden chopsticks, or the stub of a candle. You can also buy bags of fatwood online or at most places that sell wood. Fatwood is resin-impregnated pine that is made for starting wood fires (you don't want an entire fire of pine, but a little bit is good for starting fires). Don't use newspaper, lighter fluid, or anything else whose smoke you don't want to ingest. Using all-natural and chemical-free materials in your fire is what allows you to cook directly on the embers and not worry if some ash gets in your food.

First, remove the grates from the grill. (You'll add them back once the fire gets going.) Build a small pile of wood teepee-style in the firebox, so there is some space between the logs. You should always overestimate the size of your fire to ensure that there are enough coals for cooking. Light your kindling and let the fire burn, adding more logs as necessary. The flames will eventually mostly

die out, leaving glowing hot embers. At this point, you can add in coals from previous fires (any piece of wood that hasn't turned to ash is coal and can usually be reused). These coals burn very hot but burn out fast, so just mix them in, as opposed to using all coals. Once the wood starts to burn down and some starts turning to embers, you can replace the grill grates. You generally want to start cooking when your fire is about half embers and half still-flaming wood; this should take 20 to 30 minutes.

As the wood burns, lay some logs on the periphery of the grill to "roast" them. Although your wood should already be dry, when you pre-roast the logs (not so hot that they start burning, although some singed edges are okay), they will ignite in seconds rather than minutes, once they are added to the fire. Roast them like they're food, by "cooking" them on all sides. Roasted wood allows you to obtain very high heat and flames almost instantly.

Some fancy grills have wheels or levers that raise the grill grates up and down. I find it's easier and more fun to just nudge the embers closer to or farther from your cooking surface using tongs or a small log—it's the exact same concept, with no chance of the mechanism breaking. This is another place where wood has an advantage over charcoal, since nudging white-hot charcoal briquettes can give you a faceful of ash. Think of your tongs as an extension of your arms and of nudging embers like turning the dial on the stovetop. The wide, shallow, and open design of this grill makes it easy to create separate heat zones and to subtly adjust the heat while you cook.

Your high-heat zone should have embers 1 to 2 inches from the cooking surface, with occasional flames licking it. The embers for a medium-heat zone should be 3 to 5 inches from the cooking surface. All the recipes in this book call for building a high- or medium-heat fire, but by moving the embers as well as the food, any heat level is possible within seconds, much like on a stovetop. Don't get hung up on temperature levels and heat zones. As you gain grill experience, you'll quickly get a sense for when it feels as if it needs to be a little hotter or cooler. Play with some halved onions to see how different heat levels affect them (over high heat, you should get deeply colored grill marks on an onion within 3 minutes). When you grab your oiled rag with tongs to rub it over the grill grates, it should sizzle and smoke right away.

Always err on the side of heat. You might expect that meat becomes overcooked when the heat is too high, but the opposite is true. Smoldering coals (and gas and electric grills set on high) don't create sufficiently high heat to develop a flavorful crust before overcooking your steak. If you're worried about something burning, just remove it briefly with tongs or slide it to a less-hot part of the grill. And if you need to speed up cooking, you can always put the food (in a pan or not) under the grates, directly on the embers.

I never use lids since, while they can raise the heat on gas grills, they lower the heat when used with charcoal and wood. They also create moisture, acting more like a steamer than a makeshift oven. If you want to trap heat briefly at the top of your food—to melt cheese on a burger, for example—just flip a pot or pan over it.

When you're done cooking, let the embers completely burn out. Embers can stay hot (that is, flammable) for 24 hours, so just leave them in the grill until then or transfer them to a metal bucket. If you need to extinguish the fire and clean the grill before then, douse the embers with water. You can actually save embers that are still intact and don't fall apart when you bang them against something, to use for your next fire. They will dry out quickly, and you can mix them in with new firewood. Dispose of ash in a metal bucket. Wood ash is alkaline, and— especially if you have naturally acidic soil—you can spread small amounts directly on lawns, around some vegetables (tomatoes love it), or in the compost pile. Brush and wipe the grill clean and rub all surfaces with an oiled rag. If you don't mind getting water and wet ash around your grill area, you can also hose the grill down, wipe it dry, and oil it.

Grilling is all about confidence, not mastery. If you can light a sparkler, you can light a wood fire. The very first time you build a wood fire on a grill, you will eat delicious food. You'll get more confident each time you do it, and your food will get even better.

# The Plancha

A plancha is simply a large flat griddle. I use my plancha a lot, and I encourage you to have the ironworker make one for you. Or you can buy a huge cast-iron griddle, which is essentially the same thing. A plancha sits directly on the grill grates. You can get by with a huge frying pan, but it's not quite the same. A plancha is used for cooking things that are too small or too delicate for the grill grates or for things you want to sizzle in oil. It's great for scallops, whole fish, small fruits and vegetables, tortillas and bread dough, or even pancakes and eggs. I use a plancha for the Butterflied Grouper (page 98), Filet Mignon with Herb Mayo (page 184), for grilling tiny baby vegetables that might otherwise fall through the grill grates, and for toasting large quantities of chiles, spices, and nuts.

# Equipment List

Most of the time, I just head outside in a T-shirt and shorts, with tongs in one hand and two stainless-steel bowls in the other (one for raw meat, one for cooked). But to fully take advantage of the outdoor kitchen, here are the basics that you'll want to keep on hand.

### Long, sturdy tongs

Tongs are an extension of your hands, and the longer and sturdier, the better. Use them to move food as well as embers, and to transfer food off the grill.

### Cotton rags

Paper towels don't cut it near a live fire. I have a revolving cast of stained and worn-out rags that look awful in our indoor kitchen but are perfect for the grill.

### Vegetable oil in a squirt bottle

Putting oil in a squirt bottle lets you use it more judiciously. Reach for the bottle when coating pans or when moistening dried-out meat or veggies.

### Cast-iron griddle or plancha

See "The Plancha" (page 30).

### Cast-iron skillets

Cast-iron cookware is the workhorse of the outdoor kitchen. Besides using it on the grill top, you can also set it directly on the embers for an extra-strong blast of heat. If you don't want to season it yourself, you can buy preseasoned cast iron, which is a good starting point for the further seasoning that will develop quickly with frequent use. You will need at least three cast-iron skillets; the 8 inch, 12 inch, and 15 inch are the sizes I use the most, but any sizes are useful—the more the better. And don't worry about cooking acidic food like tomato sauces in them. Acidic food in a well-seasoned cast-iron pan won't take on a faint metallic flavor until after at least an hour of cooking (and the iron is good for you). Lodge is the most common (and, arguably, best-made) brand, but you can also often find good-quality seasoned cast-iron cookware at thrift stores and garage sales.

### Dutch oven

Anything between 4.5 and 6 quarts with a lid is a good all-purpose Dutch oven size. I prefer non-enameled cast iron, but enameled cast iron—like Staub or Le Creuset—works, too; it will just get beaten up. I like having a dedicated Dutch oven for the grill that I don't have to worry about getting scuffed up. Besides using it for soups, sauces, stews, and deep-frying, sometimes after a meal I'll use any leftover bones and carcasses to make a stock, while the fire slowly dies down.

### Cast-iron saucepan

Like skillets, the more cast-iron saucepans the better, but I find I rarely need more than a 3-quart saucepan.

### Stainless-steel mixing bowls

These are light but heatproof and ideal for tossing ingredients with oil and salt before grilling, holding grilled veggies to steam in their own heat, and carrying ingredients to the food processor or blender.

### Large sturdy whisk

I like a French whisk, also called a sauce whisk, rather than the more common balloon-style whisk. Although they're almost identical, the French whisk is a little sturdier, with a narrower end that can better reach the corners of pans.

### Large metal spatula

A spatula is good to have for flipping large pieces of meat or for more delicate things like fish fillets.

### Wooden spoons

Some people are nervous about using wooden spoons over a live fire. It's okay—the spoon won't spontaneously ignite. Wooden spoons are also best for seasoned cast iron, since they won't scratch the seasoning.

### Metal strainers (one fine, one medium)

A medium-mesh strainer is for the general draining of solids from liquid and for soups and sauces where you want to keep a bit of texture. A fine-mesh strainer is used mostly for broths, sauces, purees, and thin soups that you want to be uniform and silky-smooth. (Pro-tip: Several layers of cheesecloth in a medium-mesh strainer is a good substitute for a fine-mesh strainer.)

### Instant-read meat thermometer

With enough grilling experience, you'll soon get confident enough to be able to tell the degree of doneness by feel. Until then, an instant-read meat thermometer is indispensable.

### Cooling rack

A sturdy heatproof cooling rack isn't just good for holding food after cooking; you can also put it directly over the grill in case the food you're holding cools down more than you wanted it to.

### Cutting board

A big cutting board with a channel for juices is crucial for resting meat before slicing.

### Cordless immersion blender

These types of blenders were invented for the outdoor kitchen—it's great to be able to blend on the grill top without having to run into the kitchen.

### Heat-resistant welder's gloves (optional)

These gloves aren't essential, since your tongs will keep your hands out of the fire, but I like having them on hand to move embers around manually and to handle hot food.

### Ash can and scoop

Embers and ashes can stay flammable long after the fire dies down. A big ash can (I use a 6-gallon galvanized steel trash can) lets you get embers and ashes out of the way so you can clean the grill, and it lets intact embers cool down for future use.

### Fire extinguisher or bucket of water

Having one on hand can't hurt.

### Matches

Don't forget the matches.

# Part Two

# Recipes

The key to great grilling is experience. The more you cook over a wood fire, the better you'll understand how to manage the fire and what constitutes doneness. All of the recipes that follow are cooked over medium or high heat. In fact, your grill will have a range of heat zones, and you'll soon get a feel for whether your cooking needs to move to a hotter or cooler part of the grill or if you need to nudge more embers under it or pull some embers away. As I mentioned before, always err on the side of heat— you'll always be more successful cooking over a grill that's too hot than one where you struggle to get a sizzle.

The cooking times given here are very rough estimates, since every fire is different. That's why an instant-read meat thermometer is important to gauge the meat's doneness (keep in mind that the temperature will rise as meat rests); otherwise, you can go by look and feel. My recipes are very forgiving; if your food goes a little under or over, it will still taste great.

In these recipes, I refer a lot to things being "charred." There's a fine line between "charred" and "unpleasantly burnt," but it's an important one. Charring is all about balance. When you char food, you are burning it, but only in spots, so there's a balance between the bitterness of a burnt surface and the sweetness of more gentle browning, or caramelization. Think of wood-fired pizza with its mottled crust, the speckled top of a crème brûlée, the burnt ends of a fatty brisket, or the blackened tips of fire-roasted cauliflower. Don't be afraid of a little burning: there is a long time between when something develops a charred crust and when it becomes completely carbonized and turns to ash. The sweetness of fruits and vegetables under a burnt surface gives a beautiful balance, as does tender meat under a blackened crust.

## A Note on Ingredients

I salt almost everything before it hits the grill. By salting and letting it sit before placing it on the grill, you're essentially doing a quick "dry brine" (see page 131). My salt is usually fine sea salt or flaky Maldon salt. Kosher salt is good, too, especially when you need a large quantity. Whatever you use, make sure the grind isn't so coarse that it falls off anything you try to season.

At home, I use what I call butcher's salt, a mix of 50 percent salt and 50 percent freshly ground black and green peppercorns (dried green peppercorns are easy to find at spice shops or online). I always have this mixture in a little dish, and I sprinkle

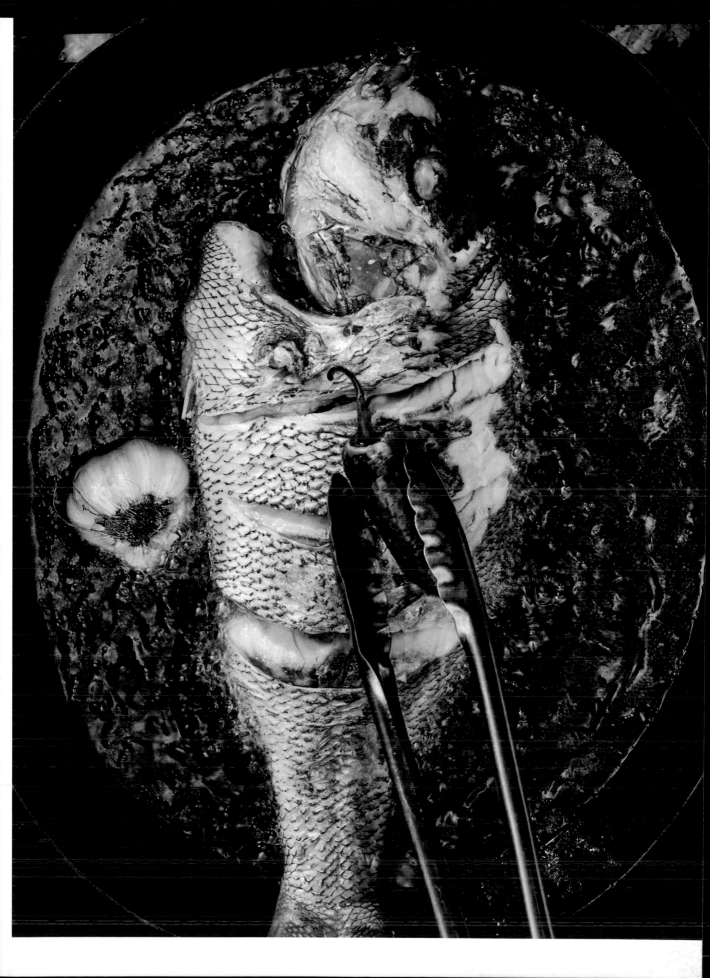

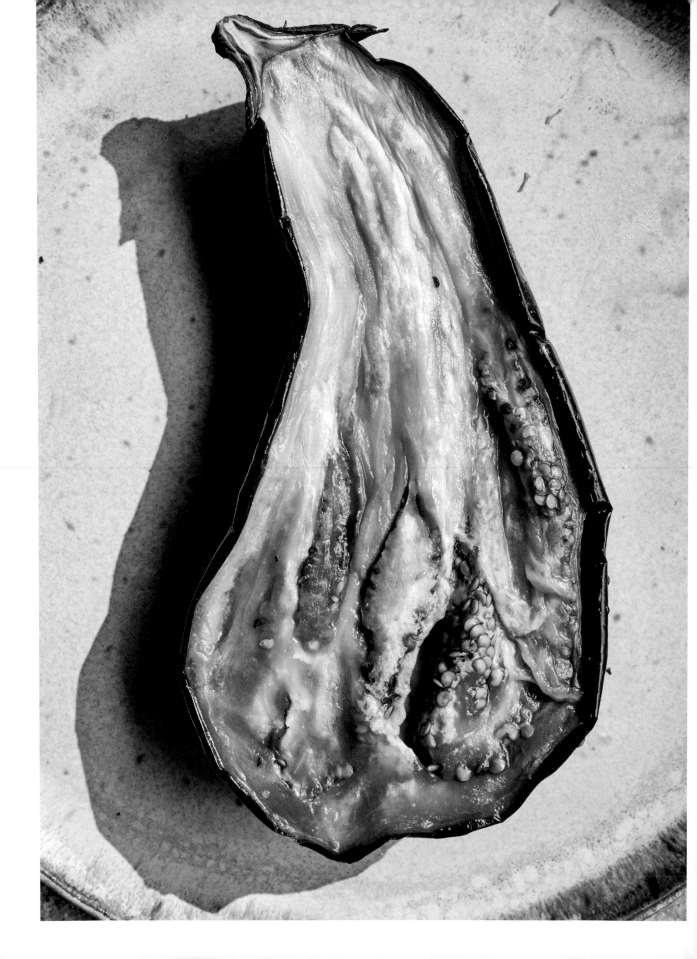

it on meat from up high, which helps it coat more evenly. The Porterhouse Steak with Butcher's Salt (page 193) really highlights the subtly unique flavor that the green peppercorns give the butcher's salt, but in other recipes, you can season with butcher's salt or just salt and pepper. Pepper is always freshly ground black pepper, unless otherwise noted.

When I call for oil in the recipes, I'm talking about extra-virgin olive oil. For cleaning the grill with an oiled rag, I use cheap vegetable oil. For vinegar, I usually use cider vinegar, or white vinegar if I want something clear.

I prefer red or white onions to yellow, since yellows are more pungent, with a higher sulfur content. However, yellow onions work fine if they're being cooked to mush, as when ember-roasting onions or blending into long-cooked sauces. And I always use unsalted butter, so I can better control the salt in the dish.

You'll notice that I almost always use honey as a sweetener in place of white or brown sugar. I think honey has a more complex flavor, it dissolves quickly in sauces and marinades, it acts as a "glue" in rubs, and it even works as a basting liquid on its own, especially for pork and chicken. The liquid in honey also helps prevent it from burning as quickly as sugar, and it has a more pleasant taste when it does burn. When I do call for sugar, it's plain white granulated sugar, unless otherwise noted.

Use long, sturdy tongs to manipulate food as it cooks (as well as nudge the embers), and to transfer food from the grill. This will help to keep you a safe distance from the intense heat and occasional flare-up of the grill.

Besides a refrigerator, the only "indoor" equipment you will need for some of these recipes is a food processor or blender. Buy a long outdoor extension cord to hook it up so you don't have to leave your grill or your guests.

# Vegetables & Sides

Cauliflower is one of the best vegetables to grill. It can stand up to high heat, its flavor improves tenfold when it's deeply browned or charred (it's almost impossible to burn), and it goes with almost any of the sauces in this book. The beer-raisin glaze couldn't be more simple, but it has incredible complexity. The raisins' sweetness is offset by the savory depth of the chiles and the reduced beer. Use a malty, rather than hoppy, beer—a porter, stout, or Scotch or Belgian ale—since a very bitter beer can taste even more bitter when reduced. I developed this sauce to serve with lamb T-bones, but lately I've been liking it just as much with thick cauliflower steaks.

Wipe the grill grates with oil to prevent sticking. Build a two-zone fire. Your high-heat zone should have embers 1 to 2 inches from the cooking surface, with occasional flames licking it. To create your medium-heat zone, nudge the embers 2 to 3 inches lower than that.

To make the glaze: Combine the raisins, chiles, beer, butter, and salt in a saucepan over high heat and bring to a boil. Move the pan to medium heat and simmer until the liquid has thickened and is syrupy, about 20 minutes. Remove from the heat and discard the chiles. Set aside.

Meanwhile, trim the leaves and stem from a cauliflower and place it stem side up on a cutting board. Starting where the florets attach to the core, slice vertically at 1-inch intervals; you should end up with two or three "steaks" and loose florets from either end (reserve these for another purpose, such as adding to a salad or grilling as a side dish for another meal). Repeat with the other cauliflower.

Rub the cauliflower steaks with the oil and season with salt and pepper. Place directly on the grill grates over high heat and cook until well charred in spots, about 4 minutes, then flip and repeat on the other side. Move to medium heat and cook for another 5 to 10 minutes, turning often. Cauliflower is done when a fork pierces it easily.

Serve with a drizzle of the glaze, making sure each serving gets a few raisins.

# Cauliflower Steaks with Beer-Raisin Glaze

Serves 4

**Beer-Raisin Glaze**

1 cup raisins (any type)

3 mulato or ancho chiles, stemmed and seeded

Two 12-ounce cans dark beer

2 tablespoons butter

1 teaspoon salt, plus more for seasoning

2 large heads cauliflower

Oil, for coating

Pepper, for seasoning

# Crudités with Grilled Green Goddess Dip

Serves 6 to 8; makes
about 2 cups of dip

For an outdoor dinner, most people would expect you to serve grilled vegetables with a straightforward dip, but here I've done something slightly more unexpected and paired barely-cooked vegetables with a grilled dip. Put some effort into crudité shopping; there's nothing worse than a crudité plate that looks as if you just took the plastic off a supermarket party platter. Some veggies I like to include are jicama, fennel, endive, asparagus, and snap peas, but usually I try to go to the farmers' market the same day and just buy whatever's the freshest and most interesting.

### Grilled Green Goddess Dip

2 ripe avocados

Oil, for coating

5 large tomatillos, peeled and rinsed

2 jalapeño chiles, stemmed, halved lengthwise, and seeded

2 tablespoons roasted garlic (see page 106)

Juice of 2 limes (about ¼ cup)

1 cup basil leaves

1½ teaspoons salt

An assortment of lightly charred vegetables, such as asparagus, jicama, fennel, snap peas, mushrooms, cherry tomatoes, baby carrots, and endive, for serving

Wipe the grill grates with oil to prevent sticking. Build a medium-heat fire. Your medium-heat zone should have embers 3 to 5 inches from the cooking surface.

To make the dip: Cut the avocados in half and remove the pits. Cut again so the avocados are quartered. Keeping the skin on, coat the flesh sides with oil and grill each flesh side over medium heat for about 60 seconds, or until there are nice grill marks. Set aside.

Coat the tomatillos and jalapeños with oil and grill over medium heat on all sides until charred but not blackened, about 5 minutes total.

Remove and discard the skins from the avocados. Add the avocados, tomatillos, jalapeños, garlic, lime juice, basil, and salt to a blender and puree until very smooth. The dip can be made up to 2 days in advance and stored, covered, in the refrigerator.

Cut the larger vegetables, such as fennel and jicama, into pieces that are slightly larger than bite size and keep the smaller vegetables, such as asparagus, mushrooms, cherry tomatoes, baby carrots, and endive, whole.

Arrange the vegetables on a platter and serve with the dip.

# Green Rice with Charred Broccoli

Serves 4 to 6

Using a pot on the grill—for soups, sauces, rice, and pasta—gives people a great sense of grilling accomplishment. This dish is packed with herbs and broccoli, which lighten it up. It almost feels more like a vegetable dish or salad than a starchy rice dish.

Transferring the charred broccoli to a tightly covered bowl lets it steam in its own heat. It's a great technique for any vegetables that don't always cook through on the grill, such as broccoli, cauliflower, green beans, and carrots.

6 large tomatillos, peeled and rinsed

Oil, for coating

1 white onion, coarsely chopped

2 cups cilantro (leaves and stems)

1 tablespoon roasted garlic (see page 106)

2 teaspoons salt, plus more for seasoning

1½ cups water

2 cups white rice

1 bunch scallions, bases trimmed

1 head broccoli, cut in half

1 cup basil leaves, coarsely chopped

1 cup parsley leaves, coarsely chopped

Wipe the grill grates with oil to prevent sticking. Build a two-zone fire. Your high-heat zone should have embers 1 to 2 inches from the cooking surface, with occasional flames licking it. To create your medium-heat zone, nudge the embers 2 to 3 inches lower than that.

Toss the tomatillos in enough oil to coat and grill over high heat until charred, about 5 minutes, turning often to char evenly. Transfer to a blender with the onion, 1 cup of the cilantro, the garlic, salt, and water and puree until smooth. Set aside.

Coat a small heavy pot or Dutch oven with oil and place over medium heat. Add the rice and cook, stirring constantly, until toasted and slightly translucent, about 3 minutes. Pour in the tomatillo puree and stir to combine. Cook, stirring only if necessary to avoid burning, until most of the liquid has been absorbed, 10 to 12 minutes. Cover and cook for 5 more minutes. Keeping the lid on, remove from the grill and let it sit and steam until ready to serve.

While the rice cooks, toss the scallions and broccoli in enough oil to coat and grill over medium heat until charred but not burned, about 1 minute for the scallions and 5 minutes for the broccoli (lay the scallions crosswise on the grill grates). Remove from the grill and place both in a bowl, tightly cover, and let steam for 5 to 10 minutes.

Coarsely chop the scallions, broccoli, and the remaining 1 cup cilantro. Add to the rice together with the basil and parsley. Fluff with a fork, season with salt, and serve immediately.

This recipe gives you BBQ-y flavors without actually barbecuing. It has the flavor of a long-cooked condiment, but it takes just 5 minutes and is foolproof—I even surprised myself how good this turned out. When I tested it on my then-seven-year-old daughter, she said, "This tastes like BBQ sauce." The #1 judge of my food is my daughter, because I get straight honesty. These onions are good anywhere you might think of using BBQ sauce.

# Honey-Chipotle Onions

Makes about 2 cups

Build a medium-heat fire. Your medium-heat zone should have embers 3 to 5 inches from the cooking surface.

Toast the chipotles in a dry skillet over medium heat until fragrant, 3 to 5 minutes. Grind to a powder in a spice grinder, then place in a bowl with the onions and salt and mix very well.

In another bowl, stir together the vinegar, lime juice, and honey until the honey dissolves.

Pack the onions into a pint-size glass jar and cover with the vinegar mixture. Cover the jar and shake well to settle the onions. Refrigerate for at least 4 hours and up to 2 weeks.

2 chipotle chiles, stemmed

1 white onion, sliced paper thin

1 tablespoon salt

1 cup vinegar

½ cup freshly squeezed lime juice (from 4 limes)

½ cup honey

At Hartwood, we go through a ton of beets, so I had to come up with a way to use all the beet greens that were left over. They're good grilled, sautéed, or braised, but when I pickled them, I knew I had a winner. Now, when I'm at the grocery store, I find myself looking for beets that have the most greens rather than the biggest beets. In this dish, the beets are earthy and meaty, and the pickled greens offer the same refreshing contrast that they do when served with meat. Try the pickled beet greens with Whole Fried Fish (page 104), Kielbasa (page 162), Duck Breasts (page 149), any steak, or as part of an assorted pickle plate.

# Beets with Pickled Beet Greens

Serves 4

Wipe the grill grates with oil to prevent sticking. Build a medium heat fire. Your medium-heat zone should have embers 3 to 5 inches from the cooking surface.

Cut the greens about a quarter inch from the beet and scrub the beets well. Rinse the greens and cut into 3-inch pieces, making sure to include the stems. Pack into a quart-size jar and add the sugar, salt, and enough vinegar to cover the greens. Shake to dissolve the sugar and salt. Refrigerate for at least 2 hours and up to 1 week.

Place the beets directly in the embers and roast until a knife easily passes through them, 20 to 30 minutes. Remove with tongs to a plate. With a paper towel, peel the beets and place them in a bowl. Toss the beets with the oil to coat and place them over medium heat, turning occasionally, until they char and crisp on the edges, about 10 minutes total. Cut the larger beets in half and serve with the pickled greens.

12 small- to medium-size beets with greens attached

¼ cup sugar

2 tablespoons salt

Vinegar, as needed (about 3 cups)

Oil, for coating

# INTO THE FIRE: COOKING IN THE EMBERS

Cooking food directly in the embers provides direct heat, radiant heat, and smoke all at once, like cooking in a tandoor oven. And there's no need to wrap anything in aluminum foil: a little ash from an all-natural wood fire won't hurt you.

The following whole vegetables cook beautifully in the fire:

**Eggplant**  When eggplant has blackened and collapsed, it's done. Just split it in half with a knife and use a spoon to scoop the flesh from the skin, then discard the skin.

**Winter squash**  Any winter squash is at its best when cooked this way. Pull it out as soon as a butter knife can easily pass through; longer cooking will dry it out. The skin is edible, but if it's unpleasantly blackened, just peel off most of it with your fingers. You can also scoop the flesh from the skin, as with eggplant.

**Onions**  An onion's protective skin makes it ideal for ember roasting. Cook it until it's squeezably soft when grabbed with tongs. Cut it open and rub the inside on meat as it grills or mash it and use to thicken soups, sauces, salad dressings, and dips.

**Cabbage**  Tuck small heads of green cabbage in the embers until easily pierced with a sharp knife. Peel away the burnt leaves before eating. Try a traditional wedge salad using ember-roasted cabbage instead of iceberg lettuce.

**Beets**  It's almost impossible to overcook—or burn—beets, making ember roasting an ideal cooking method. Toss 'em in the fire and forget about 'em. Peel with a paper towel.

**Potatoes**  All types of potatoes—savory or sweet—work equally well. Use the largest potatoes you can find, since they tend to shrivel up.

**Peppers**  Bell and poblano peppers can take a lot of ember abuse. When the skin turn completely black, use tongs to transfer them to a bowl, then tightly cover to steam in their own heat for 20 minutes. Peel off the skin with your fingers.

**Radicchio and endive**  These cook quickly and gain sweetness in the process. Remove when you can easily squeeze them with tongs, and just peel off the outer leaves before using.

Also try . . .

**Shellfish**  Put in-the-shell oysters, clams, or scallops on the embers until the shells open. Jumbo unpeeled shrimp can be thrown in the embers just until opaque.

**Steak**  When you're looking to impress, throw any steak on a more-or-less flat ember bed with a thick coating of butcher's salt (see page 36). Just keep the steak within easy reach of your meat thermometer probe, which ensures against overcooking.

This is one of the only recipes in the book that doesn't touch the grill, but it's here because it's such a perfect side dish for almost any grilled or smoked dish. You can usually find fresh horseradish in large supermarkets and specialty produce markets—it makes a difference in the same way fresh herbs do over dried—but you can substitute prepared horseradish in equal quantity.

Celery root is one of my favorite ingredients; it has the refreshing quality of celery in concentrated form, without being watery. Celery leaves are another way to introduce that fresh celery flavor and bulk up a salad or slaw (I find that celery from farmers' markets usually has a lot more leaves still attached than supermarket celery). And remember, think "cold slaw"—coleslaw should be served *cold*. Nothing's worse than warm mayonnaise.

# Celery Root and Horseradish Slaw

Serves 4 to 6

To make the mayonnaise: In a small bowl, whisk together the mayonnaise, mustard, horseradish, salt, and chile powder until smooth. Store, covered, in the refrigerator for up to 2 days.

To make the slaw: Place the onion in a bowl with the vinegar, sugar, and salt. Stir to dissolve the sugar and set aside to pickle for at least 30 minutes.

Using a mandoline or very sharp knife, slice the celery root as thinly as possible. Stack the slices and cut again lengthwise into thin strips. Do the same with the apple and the watermelon radishes. Immediately toss the celery root and apple with a little of the horseradish mayo to coat, so the cut surfaces don't turn brown. Add the drained pickled onions, celery leaves, herbs, mustard seeds, and the remaining mayo and toss well. Refrigerate, covered, for at least 1 hour and up to 2 days.

**Horseradish Mayonnaise**

1 cup mayonnaise

¼ cup Dijon mustard

¼ cup freshly grated horseradish (may substitute store-bought horseradish)

¼ teaspoon salt

¼ teaspoon chile powder (ground cayenne pepper or chile de árbol)

**Horseradish Slaw**

1 white onion, sliced paper thin and separated into rings

1 cup vinegar

1 tablespoon sugar

½ tablespoon salt

1 large celery root, peeled and cut in half

1 green apple

2 watermelon radishes (about 3 inches in diameter), peeled

1 cup celery leaves (may substitute parsley or chervil leaves)

1 cup coarsely chopped mixed fresh herbs, such as basil, dill, chives, and cilantro

2 tablespoons Pickled Mustard Seeds (page 154)

# Grilled Eggplant with Mole

*Serves 6 as a main dish or 12 as a side*

Mole—the complex Mexican sauce of chiles with nuts and/or seeds—is almost always paired with meat, but it doesn't have to be. Here, the nuttiness and chocolate from the mole work really well with the smokiness and meatiness of grilled eggplant.

### Mole

¼ cup coriander seeds

4 cloves

1 cinnamon stick

1 cup unsalted peanuts

½ cup raw pumpkin seeds (pepitas)

½ cup raw sunflower seeds

5 chipotle chiles, stemmed and seeded

4 guajillo chiles, stemmed and seeded

3 pasilla chiles, stemmed and seeded

2 ancho chiles, stemmed and seeded

2 ounces dark chocolate (80% cacao or higher)

1 teaspoon dried oregano

1 head roasted garlic (see page 106), cloves removed

1 white or red onion, quartered

Oil, for coating

3 ripe plantains, unpeeled

½ ripe pineapple, cored

¾ cup apple juice

¼ cup apple cider vinegar

½ cup honey

Salt, for seasoning

3 large globe eggplants

Oil, for coating

Wipe the grill grates with oil to prevent sticking. Build a two-zone fire. Your high-heat zone should have embers 1 to 2 inches from the cooking surface, with occasional flames licking it. To create your medium-heat zone, nudge the embers 2 to 3 inches lower than that.

To make the mole: In a dry cast-iron pan over medium heat, toast the following ingredients in separate batches until fragrant and starting to turn color: coriander, cloves, and cinnamon; peanuts; pumpkin seeds and sunflower seeds; all chiles. As each batch cooks, transfer to a large bowl. Add the chocolate, oregano, and garlic.

Coat the onion in oil and grill over high heat until charred on all sides and tender throughout, 5 to 10 minutes. Transfer to a small bowl and cover with plastic wrap so it steams in its own heat, then add to the large bowl.

Grill the plantains over high heat until blackened and soft, about 10 minutes. Peel and add to the same large bowl. Slice the pineapple, coat with oil, and grill over high heat until deeply caramelized and softened, about 5 minutes. Add to the same large bowl.

Working in batches, transfer the contents of the large bowl to a blender along with the apple juice, cider vinegar, and honey, and blend until very smooth, adding just enough water to keep the blades turning. Strain through a fine-mesh strainer, pushing the mixture through with a rubber spatula.

Transfer the mole to a large pan or stockpot and cook over medium heat for 15 minutes, adding more water if necessary to keep it at a saucy consistency. Season with salt before serving.

Slice each eggplant lengthwise into 1-inch-thick slices. Brush with oil and grill over medium heat until deep-brown grill marks appear and the eggplant is tender, 3 to 5 minutes per side. Serve with the mole.

Before orange carrots appeared in the 17th century, carrots were typically white, yellow, or purple. You can still find non-orange carrots at most farmers' markets, and I love how they look here on a puree of orange carrots.

If possible, buy small young carrots with the greens attached; the greens are tasty when young, especially when dragged through this puree. Turmeric is closely related to ginger, and you can use ginger here if you don't have turmeric. This dish also makes use of the vinaigrette that I always have in the fridge.

# Charred Carrots on Carrot Puree

Serves 4

Wipe the grill grates with oil to prevent sticking. Build a two-zone fire. Your high-heat zone should have embers 1 to 2 inches from the cooking surface, with occasional flames licking it. To create your medium-heat zone, nudge the embers 2 to 3 inches lower than that.

Bring a pot of salted water to a boil over high heat. Add the orange carrots and cook until soft, 10 to 15 minutes. Strain and add to a food processor with the turmeric, garlic, honey, habanero, and salt. Blend until completely smooth and season with more salt and/or honey, if needed.

Toss the young carrots in oil, salt, and pepper and grill over medium heat until nicely charred on all sides and cooked through, 6 to 8 minutes total, depending on the size of the carrots. Toss with just enough vinaigrette to coat and serve on top of the carrot puree, garnished with the nuts.

4 large orange carrots, peeled and cut into 2-inch pieces

1 teaspoon ground turmeric or 1 small knob fresh turmeric, peeled

1 teaspoon roasted garlic (see page 106)

1 tablespoon honey, plus more to taste

½ habanero chile, stemmed and seeded (use gloves or a paper towel when handling habaneros)

1 teaspoon salt, plus more for seasoning

1 pound small young carrots, mixed colors, with greens attached

Oil, for coating

Pepper, for seasoning

Cumin and Burnt Citrus Vinaigrette (page 111), to taste

3 tablespoons chopped toasted nuts (any kind of nut works here)

# Grilled Romaine with Smoked Fish Dressing

Serves 4

This is my take on a Caesar salad. The amount of smoked fish in the dressing makes it exceptionally hearty, and I serve this salad as a light entree. Lettuce is sturdier on the grill than you might think. The grilling adds richness and complexity, but the hearts of the lettuce stay crisp and refreshing. I usually serve it with the root ends still attached, but you can cut them off after grilling if you like.

**Smoked Fish Dressing**

1 egg yolk

1 tablespoon Dijon mustard

¼ cup vinegar

2 tablespoons honey

Juice of 2 lemons (about 6 tablespoons)

1 tablespoon roasted garlic (see page 106)

Salt and pepper, for seasoning

8 ounces (about 1 cup) Smoked Amberjack (page 107) or store-bought smoked trout, with skin and any pin bones removed

1 cup oil

2 large heads romaine lettuce, halved lengthwise

Oil, for coating

Salt and pepper, for seasoning

Wipe the grill grates with oil to prevent sticking. Build a high-heat fire. Your high-heat zone should have embers 1 to 2 inches from the cooking surface, with occasional flames licking it.

To make the dressing: Combine the egg yolk, mustard, vinegar, honey, lemon juice, garlic, salt, pepper, and smoked fish in a blender. Blend on high speed for about 15 seconds. With the motor running, slowly pour in the oil and blend until the dressing is thick and emulsified. Season with more salt and pepper. Set aside.

Toss the lettuce with the oil and salt and pepper and grill over high heat for about 30 seconds per side, just until the edges are charred but the lettuce isn't fully wilted. Serve immediately with the smoked fish dressing.

There are a lot of ways to cook corn on the grill, but don't overthink it—just cook it quickly and try to get some color on the kernels. I like corn that tastes like it was on the grill, charred and smoky. Corn is always best from summer farmers' markets, but since grilled corn is more about savory char than juicy sweetness, grilling is a good technique for out-of-season supermarket corn as well.

Wipe the grill grates with oil to prevent sticking. Build a two-zone fire. Your high-heat zone should have embers 1 to 2 inches from the cooking surface, with occasional flames licking it. To create your medium-heat zone, nudge the embers 2 to 3 inches lower than that.

Coat the corn with the butter and season liberally with salt and pepper. Grill over medium heat for about 2 minutes per side—6 minutes total—and then, if desired, lay over high heat just before serving to char further.

# Grilled Corn

Serves 4

4 ears of corn, shucked

Butter, at room temperature, for coating

Salt and pepper, for seasoning

# 10 THINGS TO DO WITH EXTRA GRILLED CORN

I always try to grill extra corn, since the leftovers are so versatile. If I'm grilling it for later use, I usually undercook it a little, so it doesn't dry out. Keep leftover corn on the cob tightly wrapped in plastic in the fridge and cut off the kernels just before using. Try them in any one of these ten ways:

**1. Corn ice cream**  Blend 2 cups coarsely pureed kernels into an ice cream base (using the recipe for Burnt Strawberry Ice Cream but omitting the strawberries, see page 212) before freezing.

**2. Pickled corn**  Add to a cold pickle brine (see page 75) and store, covered, for up to 1 month.

**3. Esquites (dressed corn kernels)**  Fry the kernels in butter, top with mayo, chile powder, lime juice, and Cotija or feta cheese, and serve as an appetizer or side dish.

**4. Corn soup**  Heat with Chicken Stock on the Grill (page 135), using half as much corn as stock; blend and strain out any solids and add cream if desired.

**5. Corn fritters**  Smash the kernels roughly with a fork, add 1 egg and 2 tablespoons flour per cup of corn, and pan-fry in butter or oil over high heat until golden brown on both sides.

**6. Mustard seed corn**  Fry in Toasted Mustard Seed Oil (page 154), garnish with Pickled Mustard Seeds (page 154), and serve as a side dish.

**7. Creamed corn**  Blend 2 cups kernels with ½ cup sour cream, 1 charred jalapeño chile, ¼ cup coconut water, and 2 tablespoons lime juice. Transfer to a saucepan and cook over medium heat until it has reached the desired consistency.

**8. Corn salsa**  To 2 cups kernels, add 1 diced raw or grilled ripe avocado, ½ diced red bell pepper, ½ minced red onion, 1 minced jalapeño chile, and 2 tablespoons lime juice.

**9. Corn guacamole**  Stir a generous amount of kernels into any guacamole recipe for added texture and a smoky-sweet flavor.

**10. Corn salad**  Toss the kernels with Grilled Green Goddess Dip (page 46) or Cumin and Burnt Citrus Vinaigrette (page 111).

You should always toss something in the embers when you're grilling (see sidebar, page 52). Eggplant usually takes only 15 to 20 minutes to get soft and smoky, making this an easy appetizer to pull together while you cook the rest of the meal. If you don't have a smoker, just grill the dates.

Wipe the grill grates with oil to prevent sticking. Build a two-zone fire. Your high-heat zone should have embers 1 to 2 inches from the cooking surface, with occasional flames licking it. To create your medium-heat zone, nudge the embers 2 to 3 inches lower than that.

Prepare the smoker for the dates (or you can grill the dates). If smoking, bring the smoker to between 170° and 220°F (see page 20).

Roast the eggplant in the embers, turning occasionally, until very soft, 15 to 20 minutes. Halve it lengthwise and scoop the flesh from the skin, discarding the skin. Put the flesh in a strainer and drain for a couple minutes.

While the eggplant cooks, smoke the dates for 20 minutes (alternately, grill the dates over high heat for about a minute per side). Finely chop the dates and set aside.

Put the eggplant in a bowl and mash with a fork until very smooth. Season with salt. Add the dates, walnuts, garlic oil, garlic, and lemon juice and mix well. Serve with the toasted bread.

# Eggplant Dip with Smoked Dates

Serves 6 to 8; makes about 2 cups of dip

1 large globe eggplant

½ cup pitted dates

Salt, for seasoning

½ cup toasted walnuts, finely chopped

2 tablespoons roasted garlic oil (see page 106)

1 tablespoon roasted garlic (see page 106)

1 tablespoon freshly squeezed lemon juice

Toasted pita bread or focaccia, for serving

# Eggplant with Cashew Cream

Serves 4 to 6

Nut butters are great for giving body to sauces and sides without the heaviness or greasiness of cheese or oil. Even heavy cream can make a dish feel too much like dessert. This garlicky cashew cream works as a sauce on its own; the trick is pairing it with something hearty but low-fat, since it's so rich. Enter grilled eggplant. It's meaty like steak but without the fat, and it loves a rich dressing. The cashew cream is tasty with other grilled vegetables, too, but the slight bitterness of the eggplant works better than a sweeter vegetable, since the sauce is already a little sweet.

1 cup raw cashews, soaked in water for at least 2 hours and up to 8 hours, plus ¼ cup, unsoaked, coarsely chopped

½ head roasted garlic (see page 106), cloves removed

¾ cup water

Salt, for seasoning

2 large globe eggplants

Oil, for coating

2 tablespoons black sesame seeds

¼ cup chopped mint leaves

Wipe the grill grates with oil to prevent sticking. Build a medium-heat fire. Your medium-heat zone should have embers 3 to 5 inches from the cooking surface.

Drain the cashews and add to a blender or food processor with the garlic and water. Blend until very smooth and season with salt. Set aside.

Grill the eggplants over medium heat, turning often, until lightly charred all over and a knife easily passes through, about 30 minutes total. Meanwhile, in a cast-iron pan over medium heat, toast the remaining ¼ cup cashews and the sesame seeds, tossing often, until fragrant, about 3 minutes.

To serve, place the eggplants on a platter and split lengthwise. Pour on the cashew cream and sprinkle with the toasted cashews, sesame seeds, and mint. Serve immediately.

# Pickles

I always have homemade pickles on hand, whether to serve as guests arrive, to eat with simple grilled chicken or on sandwiches, or just for an everyday snack. They're especially good with smoky grilled dishes, since they provide a little refreshment. These aren't the cucumber pickles that most Americans think of but a new way to serve almost any vegetable or fruit.

Generally speaking, I make cold or hot pickles, the difference being that cold pickles don't require heating the pickling solution, and hot do. Any vegetable you eat raw can be pickled hot or cold, but softer vegetables are better for cold pickles, so they don't get mushy. You can also grill any vegetable before pickling—just put a quick char on it over high heat for a minute or two, since you don't want it to get soft. And feel free to change up the seasonings with whatever spices and chiles you have on hand. Both types of pickles will keep several weeks in the fridge as long as they're covered with pickling liquid and kept in a tightly sealed container.

Try hot-pickling firmer vegetables that you can eat raw but would typically eat cooked, like broccoli, cauliflower, onions, carrots, asparagus, and green beans. These tend to be less-seasonal vegetables, making hot pickles good to prepare year-round. Whenever I have the grill going and am also low on pickles, I toss a pan of pickling liquid on to simmer and pour it over whatever vegetables I have on hand. A quick stovetop boil works just as well.

# Hot Pickles

*Makes about 1 quart*

Build a two-zone fire. Your high-heat zone should have embers 1 to 2 inches from the cooking surface. To create your medium-heat zone, nudge the embers 2 to 3 inches lower than that.

Combine the onion, jalapeños, garlic, oregano, coriander, vinegar, sugar, and salt in a saucepan over medium heat. Bring to a boil, then reduce the heat and simmer for 20 minutes. Using a slotted spoon, remove the onion, jalapeños, and garlic and discard.

Place the vegetables in a quart-size jar and add enough of the liquid to cover. Let it sit until the liquid cools to room temperature, then cover and refrigerate for at least 6 hours and up to 6 weeks.

1 white onion, peeled and quartered

2 jalapeños, halved

1 head of garlic, halved crosswise

1 tablespoon dried oregano

1 tablespoon coriander seeds

4 cups vinegar

1½ cups sugar

½ cup salt

4 cups vegetables, mixed or 1 variety, such as cipollini or pearl onions, cauliflower or broccoli florets, sliced carrots, shredded cabbage, halved radishes, whole green beans, or asparagus spears

Try cold-pickling lighter vegetables typically eaten raw, like whole baby zucchini, celery sticks, sliced cucumber, sliced fennel bulb, and halved peeled tomatillos or green tomatoes.

# Cold Pickles

*Makes about 1 quart*

Combine the chiles, cinnamon, allspice, vinegar, sugar, and salt in a bowl and stir until the sugar and salt dissolve.

Place the vegetables in a quart-size jar and add enough of the liquid to cover. Different vegetables will require different pickling times, but most will be ready in a day and will keep in the refrigerator for up to 6 weeks.

4 dried chiles de árbol or any hot dried chiles

2 cinnamon sticks

10 whole allspice berries

4 cups vinegar

½ cup sugar

½ cup salt

4 cups vegetables, mixed or 1 variety, such as whole baby zucchini, celery sticks, sliced cucumber, sliced fennel, halved tomatillos, or green tomatoes

# Wild Mushrooms with Chiles and Chestnuts

Serves 4

12 chestnuts

2 pounds mixed fresh wild mushrooms (such as porcini, shiitake, chanterelle, blue foot, and so on)

Salt, for seasoning

¼ cup oil

4 guajillo chiles, stemmed, seeded, and sliced into very thin rings (may substitute ancho or pasilla chiles)

Wild mushrooms are my favorite thing to grill in the fall, when there are a lot of different varieties to choose from in farmers' markets and better supermarkets. They're sturdy enough to put directly on the grill and are almost impossible to overcook. When wild mushrooms aren't available, this recipe also works for thick-sliced portobello mushrooms. The chestnuts add both a creamy texture and a subtle sweetness. You can use precooked and peeled chestnuts if you can't find fresh ones.

Wipe the grill grates with oil to prevent sticking. Build a two-zone fire. Your high-heat zone should have embers 1 to 2 inches from the cooking surface, with occasional flames licking it. To create your medium-heat zone, nudge the embers 2 to 3 inches lower than that.

Rinse the chestnuts and pat dry. Using a very sharp knife, cut an X into the flat side of each. Place directly over high heat if they're large enough not to fall through the grates; otherwise, you can nestle them directly in the embers. Roast for 20 to 30 minutes, until the shells peel back and the chestnuts are tender when pierced with a knife. Remove with tongs to a bowl, let cool, then peel and set aside.

Keep any mushrooms whole that are smaller than your fist. Cut the larger mushrooms in half. Season generously with salt and place over medium heat. Grill until they're deeply browned and tender, about 15 minutes.

Meanwhile, heat the oil in a large cast-iron pan over high heat. Add the chiles and cook until the oil turns red (remove the pan from the heat if the oil starts to burn before the mushrooms are ready). Add the mushrooms, toss well, and season with salt. Grate the chestnuts with a Microplane or the fine holes of a box grater over the tops of the mushrooms and serve immediately.

Sauerkraut is just cabbage that is pickled via fermentation. I find you can get a similar flavor and texture from a quick braise in vinegar, with an added layer of flavor from the grill. This sauerkraut is less astringent and "funky" than the kind you buy in stores and can be served as a side dish (especially with sausages or pork), as well as a condiment. It's a crucial ingredient in my Grilled Potato Salad (page 82) but you could also try it on burgers, grilled ham-and-Swiss sandwiches, as a pizza topping, or blended with sour cream for a dip.

# Quick Sauerkraut

*Makes about 2 cups*

Wipe the grill grates with oil to prevent sticking. Build a two-zone fire. Your high-heat zone should have embers 1 to 2 inches from the cooking surface, with occasional flames licking it. To create your medium-heat zone, nudge the embers 2 to 3 inches lower than that.

Cut the cabbage into four wedges. Grill over high heat until well charred on all sides, 3 to 5 minutes per side (don't worry about cooking it through).

Add the vinegar, water, fennel seeds, and salt to a sauté pan or saucepan over medium heat. Cook until the salt dissolves, then add the cabbage. Cover and cook for about 20 minutes, until the cabbage is cooked through but not mushy. Remove the cabbage with a slotted spoon and coarsely chop.

If using immediately, discard the cooking liquid.

This sauerkraut is best served on the day it's made to preserve its crunch and freshly grilled flavor; however, you can cover it with cooking liquid and refrigerate it, covered, for up to 1 month. Drain before serving.

½ head green cabbage, cored

2 cups vinegar

2 cups water

2 tablespoons fennel seeds

1 teaspoon salt

# Grilled Potato Salad

Serves 4

Quick-cooking fingerling potatoes are perfect for the grill. You can also boil them instead of cooking them in the embers.

1 pound mixed new potatoes, such as fingerlings, all roughly the same size, halved

Oil, for coating

Salt, for coating and seasoning

1 cup plain whole-milk yogurt

Juice of 2 lemons (about 6 tablespoons)

1 tablespoon Pickled Mustard Seeds (page 154)

1 tablespoon roasted garlic (see page 106)

1 teaspoon pepper

3 celery stalks, thinly sliced

½ cup chopped cornichons

½ cup celery leaves, chopped

¼ cup fresh dill, chopped

1 bunch chives, chopped

Build a medium-heat fire. Your medium-heat zone should have embers 3 to 5 inches from the cooking surface.

Toss the potatoes with oil and salt to coat and wrap in a large strip of aluminum foil. Place the foil packet directly in the embers and cook just until the potatoes are tender, using tongs to occasionally move the packet around so the potatoes cook evenly, about 20 minutes. Remove the potatoes from the foil and grill over medium heat, turning occasionally, until they are lightly charred, about 5 minutes total. Remove from heat and place in a large bowl.

For the dressing, whisk together the yogurt, lemon juice, mustard seeds, garlic, and pepper; season with salt. Add to the bowl while the potatoes are still warm and toss to coat. Mix in the sliced celery, cornichons, celery leaves, dill, and chives. Season with salt and serve.

Grilled zucchini gets a bad rap, yet when grilled correctly—charred and tender but not mushy—it's one of the most crowd-pleasing vegetables there is. It also takes grill marks really well. The key is to not slice it too thin—even whole zucchini are better to grill than too-thin slices.

# Grilled Zucchini with Feta

Serves 4

Wipe the grill grates with oil to prevent sticking. Build a medium-heat fire. Your medium-heat zone should have embers 3 to 5 inches from the cooking surface.

Slice the zucchini lengthwise into slices approximately 1 inch thick; large zucchini should yield two long slices (discard the thin edges) and smaller zucchini can just be cut in half lengthwise. Toss with the oil and salt and pepper. Grill on a diagonal over medium heat for 90 seconds, then turn 45 degrees and cook for another 90 seconds. Flip and repeat on the other side. Cut the zucchini crosswise on the bias into 3- to 4-inch pieces and top immediately with the feta, so the cheese softens from the heat. Squeeze the lemon on top just before serving.

4 large or 8 small zucchini

Oil, for coating

Salt and pepper, for coating

½ pound feta cheese, crumbled

2 lemons, quartered

# Broccoli Steaks with Sweet Chile Sauce

Serves 4

In this recipe, you build up a sweet-and-spicy "crust" on the broccoli "steaks," just as I encourage you to do with beef steaks and pork chops. It makes a surprising vegetarian centerpiece, but the steaks can also be "carved" at the table and served as a side dish. The chile sauce is good to have on hand in the fridge, since it's also delicious on chicken and pork.

### Sweet Chile Sauce

15 dried chiles de árbol

1 red bell pepper, stemmed, seeded, and coarsely chopped

2 cups sugar

2 cups vinegar

1 cup water

4 garlic cloves

1-inch piece fresh ginger, peeled and roughly chopped

1 teaspoon salt

4 large heads broccoli, with at least 2 inches of stem

Oil, for coating

Salt and pepper, for seasoning

Wipe the grill grates with oil to prevent sticking. Build a two-zone fire. Your high-heat zone should have embers 1 to 2 inches from the cooking surface, with occasional flames licking it. To create your medium-heat zone, nudge the embers 2 to 3 inches lower than that.

To make the sauce: Cut the stems from the chiles and roll the chiles between your fingers to shake out most of the seeds; discard the seeds. Add the chiles to a saucepan with the bell pepper, sugar, vinegar, water, garlic, ginger, and salt. Place over high heat to bring to a boil, then move to medium heat and let simmer for about 20 minutes, until it is slightly syrupy. Transfer to a blender or food processor and puree until smooth but with some small flakes of chile remaining. The sauce can be made up to 1 month in advance and stored, covered, in the refrigerator.

Prepare the broccoli by cutting away both sides vertically so that you are left with a broccoli "steak" about an inch thick (reserve the sides for another use). Coat with oil and season with salt and pepper, then grill over medium heat for 1 minute. Flip and, using a pastry brush, baste with the sweet chile sauce (don't worry if some of the sauce falls through the grill grates). Grill for a minute, then flip and baste again. Continue flipping and basting every 2 minutes or so until the sauce creates a deeply caramelized coating on the broccoli and the stem is completely cooked through, about 12 minutes total. Serve immediately.

# Grilled Escabeche with Garlicky Yogurt Sauce

Serves 4 to 6

There's something about these pickled charred vegetables tempered with creamy yogurt, heavy cream, and sweet roasted garlic that is irresistible to me. Think of this as a base recipe and feel free to use any other sturdy vegetables you have on hand, such as fennel bulbs, cauliflower, green beans, or kohlrabi. It's such an affordable, but unusual, side for any grilled dishes, and it's a good thing to make when you first light the grill. You can also mince the pickled vegetables and mix with the yogurt dressing to make a chunky sauce for fish or chicken.

### Escabeche

4 large carrots, sliced on a bias about ¼ inch thick

1 white or red unpeeled onion, halved horizontally

2 jalapeño chiles, stemmed, seeded, veins removed, and halved lengthwise

4 large radishes, halved

Oil, honey, and salt, for coating

4 cups vinegar

2 tablespoons salt

2 tablespoons sugar

4 garlic cloves

1 tablespoon dried oregano

1 cinnamon stick

### Garlicky Yogurt Sauce

½ cup plain Greek-style yogurt

½ cup heavy cream

1 tablespoon roasted garlic (see page 106)

1 teaspoon pepper

Salt, for seasoning

Wipe the grill grates with oil to prevent sticking. Build a medium-heat fire. Your medium-heat zone should have embers 3 to 5 inches from the cooking surface.

To make the escabeche: Toss the carrots, onion, jalapeños, and radishes in oil, honey, and salt to coat. Grill over medium heat until nicely charred (place the onion cut side down), about 2 minutes per side for the carrots, jalapeños, and radishes, and 5 minutes per side for the onion. As the vegetables finish cooking, use tongs to transfer them to a bowl, then tightly cover with plastic wrap to allow them to steam in their own heat.

When the vegetables are cool enough to handle, peel the onion and separate into "petals," slice the jalapeños, and cut the radish halves in half again. In a large bowl, stir together the vinegar, salt, sugar, garlic cloves, oregano, and cinnamon, until the salt and sugar dissolve. Add the vegetables, cover, and refrigerate for at least 2 hours and up to 24 hours.

Before serving, make the yogurt sauce: Whisk together the yogurt, cream, roasted garlic, and pepper in a small bowl; season with salt.

Drain the vegetables well, discarding the cinnamon stick and garlic cloves. To serve, add just enough yogurt to the vegetables to lightly coat.

These pancakes are an unexpected side dish with grilled meat and are an easy way to get used to frying on the grill. Keep the pancake mixture loose; don't pack the patties too tightly and don't press with a spatula as they cook. If you still have an indoor kitchen, these will reheat well on an ungreased baking sheet in a 400°F oven for 10 minutes.

# Sweet Potato Pancakes with Grilled Applesauce

Serves 4 to 6; makes about 2 cups of applesauce

Build a medium-heat fire. Your medium-heat zone should have embers 3 to 5 inches from the cooking surface.

To make the applesauce: Place the apples directly in the embers until they are completely soft, about 15 minutes. Remove from heat, cut the apples in half, remove the stems, pick out the seeds—no need to core—and mash with some honey, cinnamon, and salt. Serve immediately with the pancakes for the best grilled flavor. The applesauce can be stored in a covered container in the refrigerator for up to 3 days.

To make the pancakes: Using a food processor with a shredding attachment or a box grater, shred all of the potatoes and the onion. Stir in the salt. Using your hands, squeeze the liquid from the potato mixture and discard the liquid. Stir in the egg, cornstarch, and cayenne; season with salt and black pepper.

Heat about ¼ inch of oil in your largest cast-iron skillet over medium heat. Form 10 rustic patties with your hands and press gently to flatten. Cook, in batches if necessary, until browned and crisp, about 3 minutes per side. Serve immediately with sour cream and grilled applesauce, topped with the scallions.

**Grilled Applesauce**

3 apples, of any variety
Honey, to taste
Cinnamon, to taste
Pinch of salt

**Sweet Potato Pancakes**

3 sweet potatoes
1 russet potato
½ white onion

1 teaspoon salt, plus more for seasoning
1 egg
¼ cup cornstarch
1 teaspoon cayenne pepper
Black pepper, for seasoning

Oil, for frying
Sour cream, for serving
1 bunch scallions, chopped, for garnish

I don't like warm tomato soup, but gazpacho is one of my favorite things in hot weather. It cleans the palate but is still satisfying on its own. This version has the freshness of a traditional gazpacho with the depth of open-fire grilling. Use the largest tomatoes you can find for grilling.

# Grilled Tomato Gazpacho

Serves 4

Wipe the grill grates with oil to prevent sticking. Build a medium-heat fire. Your medium-heat zone should have embers 3 to 5 inches from the cooking surface.

Toss the onion, jalapeño, bell peppers, and half the tomatoes in the oil and salt (choose the largest tomatoes for this stage). Grill over medium heat, turning often, until nicely charred all over, about 5 minutes for the jalapeño and tomatoes and 10 minutes for the onion and bell peppers. As the vegetables finish cooking, use tongs to remove them from the grill. Transfer the bell peppers and jalapeño to a bowl, then tightly cover with plastic wrap to allow them to steam in their own heat for about 15 minutes. Using your fingers, peel as much skin as possible from the bell peppers and remove the stems, seeds, and veins.

Add the peppers and jalapeño to the jar of a blender along with the onion, grilled tomatoes, the remaining fresh tomatoes, the cucumber, garlic, vinegar, honey, and black pepper. Blend until smooth, then add more salt, vinegar, honey, or black pepper, if needed. Serve with a drizzle of oil. The soup can be prepared a few days ahead and refrigerated up to 5 days, but I think it's best eaten within 24 hours.

1 white or red onion, halved

1 jalapeño chile

2 red bell peppers

2 pounds mixed heirloom tomatoes

Oil, for coating

Salt, for coating and seasoning

1 cucumber

2 garlic cloves

1 tablespoon sherry vinegar, plus more to taste

1 tablespoon honey, plus more to taste

Black pepper, to taste

Extra-virgin olive oil, for finishing

# Grilled Winter Squash Soup with Pumpkin Seed Pesto

Serves 4

This is an obvious soup to make in winter, but I make it year-round since winter squash is so widely available any time of the year. Grilling squash is really satisfying because it gives such depth of flavor. I find that oven-roasting or braising squash mostly just brings out its sweetness, while grilling brings out its more savory qualities as well. You could also make this soup with squash roasted whole in the embers, but I like the texture, color, and flavor that grilling over an open flame gives the soup.

### Pumpkin Seed Pesto

½ cup toasted pumpkin seeds (pepitas)

1 cup cilantro (leaves and stems)

1 garlic clove

Zest of 1 lime

½ teaspoon cayenne pepper

Oil, as needed

### Squash Soup

3 pounds winter squash, such as butternut, acorn, or kabocha

Oil, for coating

Salt, for coating and seasoning

2 cups coconut milk, plus more as needed

1 cup coconut water, plus more as needed

1 tablespoon honey, plus more to taste

1 teaspoon ground turmeric or 1 small knob fresh turmeric, peeled

Wipe the grill grates with oil to prevent sticking. Build a medium-heat fire. Your medium-heat zone should have embers 3 to 5 inches from the cooking surface.

To make the pesto: Place the pumpkin seeds, cilantro, garlic, lime zest, and cayenne in a food processor and pulse until coarsely chopped. With the machine still running, add the oil until the mixture comes together in a "pesto" consistency. The pesto can be stored in a covered container in the refrigerator for up to 3 days.

To make the soup: Slice the squash into pieces about an inch thick; discard the seeds. Toss the pieces in the oil and salt to coat and grill over medium heat for about 5 minutes per side, or until the pieces can be easily pierced with a fork. Use tongs to transfer the pieces to a bowl, then tightly cover with plastic wrap to allow them to steam in their own heat for about 15 minutes.

Transfer the squash to a blender. Add 1¾ cups of the coconut milk, the coconut water, honey, and turmeric, and blend until smooth. Add more coconut milk or coconut water if you want a thinner consistency, but be sure you have the remaining ¼ cup of the coconut milk reserved for garnish. Add more salt and/or honey, if needed, and transfer the mixture to a saucepan to keep warm over a cooler part of the grill. Serve the soup with a dollop of pesto and a drizzle of the reserved ¼ cup coconut milk.

There are two persistent myths about asparagus. One is that the woody bases have a "natural" snapping point that you can find with your fingers. I find that wastes too much asparagus, so I just cut the ends off where they stop being green. The other myth is that thinner asparagus is better; in fact, fatter stalks are usually more flavorful, and, of course, they work better on a grill, where the outsides develop a char and the middles stay crisp and juicy.

Grilled asparagus spears are good on their own, but I love them with eggs. Sometimes I top them with fried eggs but more often with my simple gribiche, a classic French cold egg sauce.

Wipe the grill grates with oil to prevent sticking. Build a high-heat fire. Your high-heat zone should have embers 1 to 2 inches from the cooking surface, with occasional flames licking it.

Cut the bases from the asparagus spears where the green starts to fade to white, then toss with the oil and salt and pepper. Place over high heat, turning occasionally, until charred and tender, about 3 minutes total. Serve immediately, topped with the gribiche.

# Grilled Asparagus with Gribiche

Serves 4

1 pound asparagus, the fatter the better

Oil, for coating

Salt and pepper, for coating

Gribiche (page 172), to taste

# Ember-Roasted Onion Salad

*Serves 4*

Ember-roasted onions are great on their own, mashed into sour cream, pureed into dips, or used in any number of other ways. They're put to good use in this pretty salad, where the escarole is a supporting player to the onions, rather than vice versa. The escarole is sturdy enough that this salad can be made up to a couple hours in advance.

4 small unpeeled
red onions

1 bunch thyme

Juice of 2 limes
(about ¼ cup)

¼ cup oil

Salt, for seasoning

1 head escarole

Honey, to taste

Wipe the grill grates with oil to prevent sticking. Build a two-zone fire. Your high-heat zone should have embers 1 to 2 inches from the cooking surface, with occasional flames licking it. To create your medium-heat zone, nudge the embers 2 to 3 inches lower than that.

Place the onions in the embers and cook, turning occasionally, until they can be easily pierced with a sharp knife, about 30 minutes. Transfer with tongs to a bowl. When the onions are cool enough to handle, squeeze them from their skins, keeping any juices in the bowl, then separate into "petals." Place the thyme over high heat just until charred and fragrant (this will only take a few seconds). Remove from the heat, strip the leaves from the stems, and add them to the bowl. Add the lime juice and oil and season with salt. Set aside.

Place the escarole over high heat and cook just until the edges are charred but the inside leaves are still crisp, about 1 minute per side. Remove from heat and tear the leaves roughly into the bowl. Toss the salad, add more salt and/or honey, if needed, and serve.

This is a good example of how Mexican ingredients find their way into my everyday cooking. The simple tahini dressing gains a ton of complexity and subtle heat from roasted poblano chiles, balanced by a little sweetness from the raisins. It turns simple grilled artichokes into a special and unusual appetizer, but the sauce is also great on grilled cauliflower, squash, carrots, or beets.

# Artichokes with Poblano Chile Sauce

Serves 4

Wipe the grill grates with oil to prevent sticking. Build a medium-heat fire. Your medium-heat zone should have embers 3 to 5 inches from the cooking surface.

To make the sauce: Toss the poblanos in oil to coat and grill over medium heat, turning occasionally, until blackened all over, about 15 minutes total. Use tongs to transfer to a bowl, then tightly cover with plastic wrap to allow them to steam in their own heat for 20 minutes. Using your hands, peel away and discard as much charred skin, seeds, and veins as possible (it's okay if some remain). Transfer to a blender along with the oil, raisins, tahini, lime juice, yogurt, and salt and blend until smooth. Add more salt or lime juice, to taste. The sauce can be made up to 3 days in advance and stored, covered, in the refrigerator. Whisk until smooth before using.

Trim the artichokes by cutting the pointy tips from each petal. Cut the top ¼ inch from each artichoke; this will expose some purplish leaves at the center of the artichoke. Using a spoon, remove the purple leaves and scrape the centers to remove the hairy substance (the "choke") at the core. Cut the artichokes in half lengthwise and put in a bowl of water with a little vinegar to prevent discoloration.

When you're ready to grill, pat the artichokes dry, toss with oil and salt, and place them cut side down over medium heat. Cook until nicely charred and soft, about 5 minutes per side. Use tongs to transfer to a bowl, then tightly cover with plastic wrap to allow them to steam in their own heat for 15 minutes. Serve with the poblano sauce alongside.

**Poblano Chile Sauce**

2 poblano chiles

¾ cup oil, plus more for coating

¼ cup raisins

2 tablespoons tahini

Juice of 1 lime (about 2 tablespoons), plus more to taste

2 tablespoons plain Greek-style yogurt

1 teaspoon salt, plus more for seasoning

4 large artichokes

Oil and salt, for coating

Vinegar or lemon juice

# Fish & Seafood

# Butterflied Grouper

Serves 2

To me, a person who can confidently grill a large whole fish has reached a special level of grill mastery. Grouper has a firm, steak-like quality, so it won't completely fall apart on the grill, but keeping *any* whole fish in one piece on the grill takes confidence. You can use a fish cage the first couple times if you're nervous, but I encourage you to buy extra-small fish and just practice sometime when you have the grill fired up for something else. You can always make fish tacos if the fish completely falls apart.

I fell in love with grilled whole grouper while in the Yucatán, where it's pretty common, but you can substitute whole snapper, striped bass, or branzino.

One 2- to 3-pound
whole grouper,
scaled and gutted
Oil and salt, for coating

Oil the grill grates liberally to prevent sticking. Build a high-heat fire. Your high-heat zone should have embers 1 to 2 inches from the cooking surface, with occasional flames licking it.

Ask your fishmonger to remove the backbone, or you can do it yourself. To remove it yourself, place the fish skin side up on a cutting board, with the cavity spread open. Run a sharp knife along both sides of the spine from head to tail, releasing the flesh from the spine without cutting through the skin. Use kitchen shears to remove the backbone.

Rub the fish on both sides with oil and salt. Place the fish skin side down over high heat. Top with a cast-iron pan or plancha to weight it down. Allow to cook for 2 to 3 minutes, or until the fish easily lifts from the grill and has nice grill marks. Watch the tail and the head, since they can snap off and you don't want to lose them. Using tongs and a thin metal fish spatula—or two metal spatulas—flip the fish onto an oiled sizzling plancha (or sauté pan large enough to hold the fish) and cook, flesh side down, for another 2 to 3 minutes. Check to make sure the fish is cooked through, then transfer to a platter and serve.

Yes, it's possible to deep-fry on a grill; in fact, it's easy. Just build a very strong fire with the embers right up against the grill grates so you can bring the oil to the proper temperature. If the oil gets too hot, it's easy to just nudge your pan to a slightly cooler part of the grill or knock some embers away from the bottom of the pan. I like using a dark beer for the batter for added color and flavor, but any beer will work.

Build a high-heat fire. Your high-heat zone should have embers 1 to 2 inches from the cooking surface, with occasional flames licking it.

To make the mayo: Combine the egg yolks and lemon juice in a blender or food processor. Blend for 30 seconds and while continuing to blend, slowly drizzle in the oil; the mixture should become thick and emulsified. Add the garlic and salt and blend just to combine. The mayo can be stored, covered, in the refrigerator for up to 3 days.

To prepare the fish: Add the oil to a high-sided cast-iron skillet or a wide Dutch oven (the oil should be at least an inch deep). Place the pan over high heat until the oil starts to ripple; it should read between 360° and 380°F on a deep-fry or candy thermometer.

Combine the flour, chile powder, salt, and baking soda in a large bowl. While whisking, add the beer slowly and continue whisking until smooth; it should have the consistency of pancake batter. Season the fish fillets with salt, coat with plain flour, and dip into the beer batter. Let any excess batter drip back into the bowl and gently lay the fish in the oil (work in batches and don't let the fish pieces touch). Fry for 2 to 3 minutes per side (use a metal spatula or slotted spoon to flip), until deep golden brown and crisp. Remove with a slotted spoon and drain on a wire rack or on a plate lined with paper towels. Serve with the garlic mayo.

# Beer-Battered Fish with Roasted Garlic Mayo

Serves 4; makes about 2 cups of mayo

**Roasted Garlic Mayo**

3 egg yolks, at room temperature

1 tablespoon freshly squeezed lemon or lime juice

1¾ cups oil

2 tablespoons roasted garlic (see page 106)

2 teaspoons salt

**Beer-Battered Fish**

5 cups oil, plus more as needed

1½ cups all-purpose flour, plus more for coating

1 teaspoon ancho chile powder

1 teaspoon salt, plus more for seasoning

½ teaspoon baking soda

One 12-ounce can dark beer

2 pounds boneless, skinless whitefish fillets, such as cod or amberjack, cut into 1½-inch-thick strips

# Salmon with Almond–Tarragon Salsa Verde

Serves 4

Due to its high fat content, salmon is hard to overcook. Some people like it rarer, and some prefer it fully cooked, so just grill it as each guest wants.

The salsa verde is my version of a chimichurri or a spicy pesto, and I usually serve it with fish or grilled cauliflower. Tarragon is such an underrated herb and is amazing with fish. Its anise-y flavor reminds me of hoja santa, an herb that is used a lot in the Yucatán.

**Almond-Tarragon Salsa Verde**

1 cup skinned unsalted almonds (whole or slivered)

1 cup tarragon leaves

½ cup Jalapeño Relish (page 162; may substitute store-bought pickled jalapeños)

Zest and juice of 2 limes (about 1 tablespoon zest and ¼ cup juice)

1 teaspoon salt, plus more for coating

1 cup oil

Four 6- to 8-ounce salmon steaks, with skin on

Oil and salt, for coating

Wipe the grill grates with oil to prevent sticking. Build a medium-heat fire. Your medium-heat zone should have embers 3 to 5 inches from the cooking surface.

To make the salsa: Toast the almonds in a cast-iron pan over medium heat until fragrant, about 5 minutes. Allow to cool, then add to a food processor with the tarragon, jalapeño relish, lime zest and juice, and salt. Blend until finely chopped, 20 to 30 seconds, then add the oil and blend for another 15 seconds, until it's well mixed but not quite smooth. Set aside.

Rub the salmon with oil and salt. Place over medium heat and cook until the fish releases from the grill grates without force, about 3 minutes. Using a thin metal fish spatula, flip and cook for another 3 minutes, until it's barely pink in the middle or it's cooked to the desired doneness. Let rest for 5 minutes before serving with the salsa.

# Whole Fried Fish

Serves 4

This is the reason you need an outdoor grill: no one wants to fry fish indoors. Outside, however, it becomes a pleasure. It doesn't stink up your kitchen, and little flare-ups from splattering oil are fun, not dangerous. Frying in a pan is also easier than grilling a whole fish directly on the grill grates and probably more impressive to your guests. Make sure you have a pan big enough to hold the fish; I use a 15-inch Lodge cast-iron pan. Cooking the vegetables with the fish flavors the oil and is also the base for a quick sauce.

4 cups oil, plus more as needed

4 garlic cloves

1 white onion, quartered

1 jalapeño chile, stemmed, halved, and seeded

One 3- to 5-pound whole fish, such as snapper, striped bass, or hogfish, scaled and gutted

Salt, for seasoning

1 bunch cilantro (leaves only)

juice of 2 limes (about ¼ cup)

Build a high-heat fire. Your high-heat zone should have embers 1 to 2 inches from the cooking surface, with occasional flames licking it.

Add the oil to your largest cast-iron skillet (the oil should be at least ¾ inch deep). Place the pan over high heat until the oil starts to ripple. Add the garlic, onion, and jalapeño and fry until the garlic is cooked through but not burnt, about 3 minutes. Use tongs to remove the garlic and set aside.

Using a sharp knife, cut 2 or 3 deep slits into both sides of the fish, being careful not to cut through the bone.

Push the onion and jalapeño to the sides of the pan and add the fish. Cook until the skin is crisp and golden brown, 5 to 6 minutes, then flip the fish with a metal spatula and cook for another 5 minutes, or just until cooked through (cut into it; the flesh should be opaque and flake with a fork). Keep stirring the onion and jalapeño as well; they should be tender and browned by the time the fish is cooked. Remove the fish with two slotted spoons and drain on a wire rack or on a plate lined with paper towels. Season with salt.

Scoop the garlic, onion, and jalapeño into a food processor or mortar and pestle and add the cilantro and lime juice. Puree until smooth, season with salt, and serve warm with the fish.

# FOUR ROADS TO ROASTED GARLIC

I use roasted garlic in everything. It adds sweetness and great depth of flavor, and its buttery texture can help thicken and emulsify all kinds of sauces and dressings. A lot of recipes call for slathering garlic heads in oil before roasting, but in Mexico, they always dry-roast garlic, and it works just fine—any method of slow-cooking garlic cloves will give you roasted garlic. Before cooking, rub away the loose, papery outer skins from the garlic heads, while leaving each clove in its individual outer skin.

Whatever your preparation method, roasted garlic can be refrigerated for up to 4 days when kept in its bulb form and wrapped tightly. You can also submerge the whole bulbs or individual cloves in olive oil—or squeeze the cloves from the skins and cover the pulp with olive oil—and refrigerate, tightly covered, for up to 10 days.

**Confit**  This is by far my favorite way to roast garlic, since you end up with roasted garlic oil, which I use for salad dressings, seasoning cooked greens, or just in place of regular oil for grilling. Slice the tops off 6 heads of garlic to expose the cloves. Place the heads cut side down in a small cast-iron skillet (so the garlic fits snugly) and add enough olive oil to completely cover the garlic. Cut a parchment paper round slightly smaller than the pan diameter and place it over the top, then cover tightly with aluminum foil. Place the pan over medium heat for about an hour, until the cloves are soft. Check it occasionally: the oil should be very hot but not bubbling, so move it to a cooler part of the grill, if necessary. Remove the garlic (store the bulbs per the above instructions) and strain the oil through a fine-mesh strainer or cheesecloth. Store the oil in a covered container in the refrigerator; you can mash a little roasted garlic pulp into it to amp up the flavor.

**Grilling**  Rub the loose papery coating from however many garlic heads you want to cook, keeping the heads intact. Place over the coolest part of the grill and roast, turning occasionally, while you prepare the rest of the meal. When the heads are done, the outside should be well charred and the cloves soft when poked.

**Ember-roasting**  Like all alliums, garlic can be cooked directly in the embers, but you may want to wrap each head in aluminum foil just to protect the outer cloves from completely burning. Place the heads in a part of the ember bed where they're not covered by embers, so they can roast relatively slowly, but be sure they're getting heat from all sides. Start checking for doneness after 30 minutes.

**Plancha**  When you just need a little roasted garlic, individual cloves can be quickly roasted on a plancha or griddle until they are charred and soft. Be sure to keep each clove encased in its outer skin when separating the cloves.

This recipe works best with a leaner fish. I use amberjack, but you could substitute grouper, pompano, or mahi mahi. The fish will come out crispy in some parts and deeply layered with smoke, while the inside will be just cooked through and still moist. The guajillo chile oil lends good flavor and color, but you can add the smoked fish to any infused olive oil—tarragon, fennel, and garlic all work well.

You can serve the fish right away, but I like keeping it in the fridge to serve as an appetizer with crackers, in smoked-fish salads, or blended into salad dressings. It's like an elevated, smoky canned tuna. It should keep for a couple weeks in the fridge as long as it's always covered with oil.

Prepare the smoker and bring to between 170° and 220°F (see page 20). Coat the amberjack with oil and salt. Smoke for 2 hours. The fish should have a deeply golden color when done. Transfer the fish to a board and set aside until cool enough to handle. Using your hands, break the fish into smaller pieces and place in a covered container.

Add the chiles to a blender together with the 1½ cups oil and 1 teaspoon salt and blend until smooth. Strain and pour over the fish to cover. Serve right away or store, covered, in the refrigerator.

# Smoked Amberjack

Serves 4

1½ pounds boneless, skinless amberjack fillets

1½ cups oil, plus more for coating

1 teaspoon salt, plus more for coating

4 guajillo chiles, toasted, stemmed, and seeded

Trout is one of the few fish that's easy to cook whole directly on the grill. It's small and manageable, and the skin is so fatty that it just wants to crisp up, and as long as the skin is cooked, it won't stick to the grill. By splaying the fish open, all the skin crisps evenly on the grill, and the trout is thin enough that the flesh cooks through without needing to be flipped. You end up with incredibly tender flesh, since it never touches the grill.

I usually have the vinaigrette in my fridge. Use it on any green salad (it completely transforms a boring kale salad) or on chicken. Toasting the cumin well and charring the citrus make a big difference in boosting the flavor.

# Rainbow Trout with Cumin and Burnt Citrus Vinaigrette

Serves 4

Wipe the grill grates with oil to prevent sticking. Build a medium-heat fire. Your medium-heat zone should have embers 3 to 5 inches from the cooking surface.

To make the vinaigrette: Add the cumin to a medium sauté pan or cast-iron skillet and shake over medium heat until toasted and fragrant, about 2 minutes. Grind until very fine in a spice grinder or blender and set aside.

Zest 1 orange and 1 lemon and set zest aside. Cut all the oranges and lemons in half and toss in about 1 tablespoon each of oil and honey, just enough to coat. Place the citrus cut side down on the grill over medium heat and grill until nicely charred and fragrant, 1 to 2 minutes. Once they have cooled, juice to get about 1½ cups juice.

Combine the juice, vinegar, shallot, orange and lemon zest, cumin, salt, oregano, and remaining 2 tablespoons honey in a bowl. Whisk, until the salt and honey have dissolved. While whisking, slowly pour in the 1½ cups oil and continue to whisk until emulsified. The vinaigrette can be stored in a covered container in the refrigerator for up to 1 week.

To cook the trout: Open and gently press each fish so it lies flat. Rub the fish with oil and salt. Place skin side down over medium heat and cook until the skin is browned and crisp and the flesh turns opaque, 4 to 5 minutes. Serve the fish folded back over (so it looks again like a whole fish).

**Cumin and Burnt Citrus Vinaigrette**

1½ tablespoons cumin seeds

3 oranges

3 lemons

1½ cups oil, plus more for coating

3 tablespoons honey, plus more for coating

¼ cup vinegar

½ shallot, grated

1½ teaspoons salt

½ teaspoon Mexican oregano

4 whole rainbow trout, 12 to 16 ounces each, scaled and gutted

Oil and salt, for coating

# Shrimp with Fermented Pineapple–Peanut Sauce

Serves 4 to 6

Shell-on shrimp are so easy to grill, since the shell helps protect them from overcooking and also adds flavor. I love pairing shrimp with tropical flavors. This foolproof sauce is a great introduction to the wonders of fermentation and doesn't take weeks of waiting. Many pineapple and other tropical-fruit salsas are just sweet, but this one has a much more complex flavor with a minimum of ingredients. It's perfect served as a dip with any seafood or with grilled chicken wings.

**Fermented Pineapple–Peanut Sauce**

1 cup roasted unsalted peanuts

10 dried chiles de árbol, stemmed and seeded

1 cup oil, plus more for coating

2 tablespoons honey, plus more for seasoning

1 tablespoon salt, plus more for seasoning

1 ripe pineapple, cored, and cut into small chunks

2 pounds unpeeled jumbo shrimp

Oil and salt, for coating

To make the sauce: Put the peanuts, chiles, oil, honey, and salt in a blender and blend until smooth. Add the pineapple, cover with plastic wrap, and place in the sun or in a warm area of your kitchen for at least 3 hours, or until the liquid begins to bubble. Blend the mixture until smooth, then transfer to a medium-mesh strainer or cheesecloth and push through with a rubber spatula, discarding the solids. Season with more salt and/or honey, if needed. Store, covered, in the refrigerator for up to 2 weeks.

Wipe the grill grates with oil to prevent sticking. Build a medium-heat fire. Your medium-heat zone should have embers 3 to 5 inches from the cooking surface.

Using scissors, cut through the backs of the shrimp shells and remove the dark vein with a small knife (this will also make it easier to peel the shrimp). Toss the shrimp with oil and salt and place over medium heat. Grill just until opaque, 3 to 4 minutes per side (check by cutting into one, and remove the shrimp from the heat the minute they're no longer translucent in the middle). Serve the shrimp whole with the sauce drizzled on top or passed alongside.

Even when I'm not in Mexico, I still like to make ceviche for my friends and family. It's an easy appetizer that almost everyone loves. Cucumber is a great addition to ceviche, lending a juicy, refreshing note that goes well with briny fish and sweet onion. Cucumbers are fun to grill in general, making a light and unexpected side dish year-round.

Wipe the grill grates with oil to prevent sticking. Build a two-zone fire. Your high-heat zone should have embers 1 to 2 inches from the cooking surface, with occasional flames licking it. To create your medium-heat zone, nudge the embers 2 to 3 inches lower than that.

To make the marinade: In a blender, combine the cucumber with the lime juice, jalapeño, basil, and salt and blend until smooth. Transfer to a fine-mesh strainer or cheesecloth over a large bowl and push the mixture through with a rubber spatula; discard solids. Set the bowl over ice to cool.

To prepare the onions: Cut the green tops from the onions. Toss the greens in oil and salt and grill over high heat for about 1 minute, just until charred, then chop coarsely and set aside. Slice the white parts of the onions as thinly as possible and place in a bowl with the 1 teaspoon salt, sugar, and enough vinegar to cover. Set aside to pickle while prepping the remaining ingredients.

To prepare the cucumber: Cut the cucumber lengthwise and remove the seeds. Toss with oil and salt and grill over medium heat just until charred, 1 to 2 minutes per side. Cut into roughly matchstick-size strips about 1 inch long.

With your sharpest knife, slice the fish at a 45-degree angle into very thin (about ⅛ inch) slices, then cut crosswise into pieces approximately 2 inches long. (Freezing the fish for about 20 minutes before slicing can make it easier to slice evenly.)

When you are ready to serve, salt the fish lightly. Add the marinade and mix well. Stir in the drained pickled onions, grilled onion greens, cucumber, chopped basil, and celery. Serve immediately.

# Grilled Cucumber, Snapper, and Spring Onion Ceviche

Serves 4

**Marinade**

1 cucumber

1 cup freshly squeezed lime juice (from about 8 limes)

1 jalapeño chile, stemmed

½ cup basil leaves

1 teaspoon salt

**Pickled Onions**

8 spring onions, white and green parts (may substitute large scallions)

Oil, for coating

1 teaspoon salt, plus more for coating

1 teaspoon sugar

Vinegar, for pickling

**Grilled Cucumber**

1 cucumber

Oil and salt, for coating

1½ pounds boneless, skinless snapper or any other whitefish

Salt, for seasoning

½ cup basil leaves, coarsely chopped

1 celery stalk, thinly sliced

# 4-Minute
# Spicy-Sweet Tuna

Serves 4

Tuna is my favorite fish to catch and cook. When I'm in Tulum, I eat it almost daily in late summer, when the fishermen bring us line-caught yellowfin tuna, a fast and strong fish, which is lean but has incredible flavor and texture. In the United States, I eat whatever variety of tuna is freshest (just ask your fishmonger), as long as it's not overfished (bluefin is a no-no) and it's fished in a way that has minimal environmental impact. You should always know where and how your fish is caught.

This recipe features my go-to rub, which works well with any firm-fleshed fish, and everyone—including the kids—clears their plates when this is dinner. The honey in the rub helps it adhere. Don't marinate for more than an hour, so the centers of the tuna steaks keep their clean, fresh flavor.

You can also serve the tuna at room temperature, sliced across the grain and set on top of a quick salad.

**Rub**

2 tablespoons salt

2 teaspoons cayenne pepper

2 teaspoons sweet paprika

1 teaspoon ground white pepper

1 teaspoon celery salt

1 tablespoon peeled and finely grated fresh ginger

1 large garlic clove, grated

2 tablespoons oil

1 tablespoon honey

Two 12-ounce tuna steaks, about 1½ inches thick

Oil, for drizzling

Lemon wedges, for serving

Wipe the grill grates with oil to prevent sticking. Build a high-heat fire. Your high-heat zone should have embers 1 to 2 inches from the cooking surface, with occasional flames licking it.

To make the rub: Mix the salt, cayenne, paprika, white pepper, celery salt, ginger, garlic, oil, and honey in a small bowl.

Cover the tuna with the wet rub, massage for about 3 minutes, then refrigerate uncovered for 30 to 60 minutes.

When you are ready to cook, place the tuna steaks on the grill grates, with at least 2 inches between them. (You want the space so the oil in the rub will drip down and kick up more flames, helping to create a crust while the tuna remains medium-rare.)

Using a thin metal fish spatula, flip the tuna after 2 minutes, being careful not to let the fish flake apart. Cook for another 2 minutes. You want to check for doneness without cutting into the fish, so watch the thick edges of the fish; pink should be the dominant color.

Transfer to a cutting board and let the fish rest for 4 to 5 minutes. Slice the tuna along (not against) the grain. Tuna is a lean fish, so you can brush a little warm oil over it as it sits so it doesn't dry out. Eat it hot or store, covered, in the refrigerator for up to 8 hours. Serve cool or at room temperature. Hot or cool, drizzle it with oil and serve it with the lemon.

# Grilled Citrus and Sweet Potato Ceviche

Serves 4

Sometimes it's nice to add a starchy element to ceviche to balance out the acidity and make it more of a meal. Sweet potatoes serve that purpose, while adding a nice sweetness and vivid color. Sweet potatoes might seem unusual in ceviche, but they're common in Peruvian ceviche, which often includes *choclo*, the starchy large-kerneled Peruvian corn. I think of this as a fall or winter ceviche.

1 small fennel bulb, with fronds attached

1 teaspoon salt, plus more for seasoning

1 tablespoon sugar

Vinegar, for pickling

¼ cup oil

¼ cup honey

1 large sweet potato, sliced lengthwise into ¾-inch slices

5 limes

2 oranges

2 mandarins

1 grapefruit

1½ pounds boneless, skinless snapper or any other whitefish

½ small red onion, sliced paper thin

2 plum tomatoes, diced

½ Granny Smith apple, peeled, cored, and cut into matchstick-size batons

¼ cup chopped cilantro leaves

Wipe the grill grates with oil to prevent sticking. Build a medium-heat fire. Your medium-heat zone should have embers 3 to 5 inches from the cooking surface.

Trim root and stalks from the fennel bulb, cut into quarters, and remove and discard the core. Slice paper thin with a mandoline or sharp knife. Cut the fronds from the stalks, mince, and set aside. Combine the fennel with the salt, sugar, and enough vinegar to cover. Set aside to pickle while prepping the remaining ingredients.

Mix the oil and honey together in a large bowl. Toss the sweet potato in the oil-honey mixture to coat, letting any excess liquid drip back into the bowl. Season the sweet potatoes with salt and grill over medium heat until they are brown and caramelized and are easily pierced with a fork, about 5 minutes per side. Use tongs to transfer to a bowl, then tightly cover with plastic wrap to allow them to steam in their own heat as they cool. Once they are cool enough to handle, cut into cubes.

Set aside 2 limes and cut all the remaining citrus in half. Brush the cut sides with the remaining oil–honey mixture and place them cut side down over medium heat until they are nicely charred, about 2 minutes. Once they have cooled, juice all of them plus the 2 fresh limes that were set aside, and strain.

Cut the fish into ½-inch cubes and salt lightly. Add the citrus juice and mix well. Add the sweet potato, drained pickled fennel, onion, tomato, apple, cilantro, and 2 tablespoons of the fennel fronds. Serve immediately.

Bouillabaisse recipes can be unnecessarily complicated and dogmatic about ingredients and techniques. I probably shouldn't even call this bouillabaisse, since it doesn't have the traditional rascasse (red scorpionfish), let alone the saffron or rouille, and is more of a brothy sauté than a fish stew. But the fennel, tarragon, and garlic make me think of Provence.

# Easy Bouillabaisse with Tarragon-Garlic Toasts

Serves 4

Wipe the grill grates with oil to prevent sticking. Build a two-zone fire. Your high-heat zone should have embers 1 to 2 inches from the cooking surface, with occasional flames licking it. To create your medium-heat zone, nudge the embers 2 to 3 inches lower than that.

To make the bouillabaisse: Place the tomato directly in the embers until it blackens. Remove to a plate and set aside.

Trim root and stalks from the fennel bulb, cut into quarters, remove and discard the core, and mince. Cut the fronds from the stalks, mince, and set aside.

Heat the oil in a deep pan or Dutch oven over high heat. Add the onion, garlic, ginger, and minced fennel and cook until the vegetables are soft and golden brown, about 5 minutes. Rub most of the burnt bits off the tomato and add to the pan, crushing with the back of a spoon. Add 2 tablespoons of the fennel fronds, the tarragon, basil, fish stock, and salt and pepper. Cover and bring to a boil.

Add the clams to the pan, cover, and cook until the shells open (discard any that don't open). Place the shrimp and fish directly on the grill, over high heat, and cook just until charred on both sides. Add to the pan, cover, and remove the pan from the heat until ready to serve (the residual heat will cook the shrimp and fish within 10 minutes).

To make the toasts: Heat the oil in a small cast-iron pan over medium heat. Add the garlic and salt and cook until the garlic starts to turn golden brown. While the garlic cooks, toast the bread over medium heat until the slices are golden brown, with grill marks on both sides. Add the tarragon to the oil, stir well, and brush the slices generously with oil. Serve immediately with the bouillabaisse.

## Bouillabaisse

1 large tomato

½ small fennel bulb, with fronds attached

¼ cup oil

½ white onion, minced

4 garlic cloves, sliced

2-inch piece fresh ginger, peeled and sliced

2 tablespoons tarragon leaves, chopped

6 basil leaves, chopped

4 cups fish stock (I like Aneto brand)

Salt and pepper, for seasoning

½ pound small hardshell clams, such as littleneck or Manila, scrubbed and rinsed of all sand

½ pound unpeeled head-on large shrimp

1½ pounds boneless, skinless whitefish fillets, such as cod, sea bass, or snapper

## Tarragon-Garlic Toasts

6 tablespoons oil, plus more for brushing

3 tablespoons minced garlic

Generous pinch of salt

¼ cup minced tarragon leaves

Eight ½-inch-thick slices French bread

# Jerk-Smoked Shrimp on a Stick

*Serves 4*

This recipe makes great use of the smoker, since it cooks the shrimp relatively quickly and is a forgiving cooking method (peeled shrimp can easily overcook on the grill, but for some reason smoked shrimp almost never tastes overcooked). It's also nice to have the grill completely available for other dishes. Still, you can easily just grill the shrimp. You can also chop the shrimp and mix it with avocado, lime, and a little mayo for an interesting shrimp salad to serve on its own or pack into hot dog buns for picnic sandwiches.

The rub is kind of an American jerk seasoning. Made with cayenne instead of Scotch bonnet peppers, it's not as searingly spicy as the Jamaican version. You could also rub it on chicken or pork before grilling.

### Rub

1 tablespoon coriander seeds

1 tablespoon whole allspice berries

½ tablespoon cumin seeds

1 teaspoon black peppercorns

1 teaspoon ground cloves

1 teaspoon sweet paprika

1 teaspoon cayenne pepper

Zest of 2 limes

1 tablespoon salt

16 jumbo shrimp, peeled and deveined

Honey, as needed

4 limes, halved, for serving

Wipe the grill grates with oil to prevent sticking. Build a two-zone fire. Your high-heat zone should have embers 1 to 2 inches from the cooking surface, with occasional flames licking it. To create your medium-heat zone, nudge the embers 2 to 3 inches lower than that.

To make the rub: Combine the coriander, allspice, cumin, and peppercorns in a heavy pan and toast over medium heat until fragrant, about 3 minutes. Grind to a fine powder in a spice grinder or blender and mix in the cloves, paprika, cayenne, lime zest, and salt.

Prepare the smoker and bring to between 170° and 220°F (see page 20). Coat the shrimp liberally with the spice mixture. The shrimp's own moisture should help the rub adhere, but if not, add a little honey. Place 4 shrimp on each of 4 metal skewers (if using wood skewers, soak for an hour before using) and smoke for 30 to 40 minutes. Just before serving, place the shrimp over high heat for a minute per side to heat through. (You can also grill the shrimp without smoking; grill over medium heat for about 3 minutes per side, just until cooked through.) Grill the limes and serve with the shrimp.

Whenever I see live lobsters at the fish market, I immediately think of special occasions, something I bust out once a year to impress a group. But lobster isn't fun for everyone, since it's a hassle trying to pick every last bit of the meat from every part of the bodies. I came up with this dish as a way to enjoy lobster on a regular basis. The lobster itself couldn't be easier to grill, and the other ingredients are economical enough to make up for the cost of the lobster tails. Still, by all means use whole lobster for this if you want; substitute 2 whole lobsters and pick the meat after cooking. The charred citrus and brown butter vinaigrette is great with any hot or cold shellfish.

# Grilled Lobster and Corn Salad with Citrus–Brown Butter Vinaigrette

Serves 4

Wipe the grill grates with oil to prevent sticking. Build a medium-heat fire. Your medium-heat zone should have embers 3 to 5 inches from the cooking surface.

Toss the corn and spring onions with oil and salt and grill over medium heat until nicely charred, about 4 minutes. Toss the lobster meat with oil and salt and grill over medium heat, about 2 minutes per side or just until cooked through. As they finish cooking, transfer the vegetables and lobster to a plate and let cool to room temperature. Cut the kernels from the cobs, coarsely chop the onions, and cut the lobster into pieces about 1 inch square. Add to a large bowl, together with the chile, sliced celery, basil, dill, mint, and chopped celery leaves. Season with salt.

To make the vinaigrette: Cut the oranges and limes in half, toss with the oil and honey, and place cut side down over medium heat. Grill until charred, about 3 minutes, and transfer to a plate. Meanwhile, heat the butter in a small saucepan over medium heat until it begins to smell nutty and turn a very light brown (if it seems to be cooking too quickly, just briefly remove from the heat). Remove the pan from the heat and squeeze the citrus into it. Whisk to emulsify and season with additional honey and/or salt. Dress the lobster salad liberally with the vinaigrette and serve.

4 ears of corn, shucked

4 spring onions, white and green parts (may substitute large scallions)

Oil, for coating

Salt, for coating and seasoning

4 large lobster tails (about 8 ounces each), with meat extracted from the shells

1 serrano chile, stemmed and thinly sliced into rounds

3 celery stalks, thinly sliced on the bias

½ cup basil leaves, coarsely chopped

¼ cup dill, coarsely chopped

¼ cup mint leaves, coarsely chopped

½ cup celery leaves, coarsely chopped

**Citrus–Brown Butter Vinaigrette**

2 oranges

2 limes

Oil and honey, for coating

½ cup (1 stick) butter

# Poultry

# Butterflied Chicken with Toasted Mustard Seed Oil

Serves 4 to 6

Nothing is better than brined chicken on the grill. You don't have to stress about cooking times since the brining keeps it juicy, and the skin crisps up better—and with better flavor—than it does in an oven. Butterflying (removing the backbone so it can lie flat), whether for chicken or fish, is an especially good technique for the grill, since the food cooks evenly and quickly. It also looks beautiful on a platter.

This dish is a great showcase for the toasted mustard seed oil that I use a lot. It's a simple ingredient that's transformative. Mustard shows up a lot in BBQ recipes, but, in contrast to Dijon or other prepared mustards, this is a less in-your-face way to infuse food with its deep, spicy, earthy character. Keep basting the chicken with it as you grill—you can't have too much of it.

Two 3- to 4-pound
whole chickens

**Brine**

½ cup salt
½ cup sugar
8 cups water

Toasted Mustard Seed Oil
(page 154), for coating
Salt and pepper, for
coating

Wipe the grill grates with oil to prevent sticking. Build a two-zone fire. Your high-heat zone should have embers 1 to 2 inches from the cooking surface, with occasional flames licking it. To create your medium-heat zone, nudge the embers 2 to 3 inches lower than that.

To prepare each chicken, using kitchen shears, cut along both sides of the back bone and remove (your butcher can also do this for you). Place the chicken skin side up on the cutting board and apply firm pressure to the breastbone to flatten.

To make the brine: Combine the salt, sugar, and water and stir until dissolved. In a large bowl or stockpot, submerge the chickens in the liquid and refrigerate, covered, for at least 4 hours or up to overnight. Remove and pat dry.

Coat the chickens with the mustard seed oil, salt, and pepper and grill, bone side down, over high heat for about 10 minutes. Flip the chickens, move to medium heat, and cook for another 30 minutes, or until an instant-read meat thermometer placed in the thickest part of the thigh reads 165°F. Flip the chickens occasionally and baste with more mustard seed oil, if needed. Transfer to a cutting board and let the chickens rest for 10 minutes before carving into serving pieces.

# BRINING 101

The science behind brining is easy to research, but all you really need to know is that it enhances both moistness and flavor in meat, especially poultry and pork. As a rule, your brine solution should be ½ cup salt for every half gallon of water; I usually add an equal amount of sugar. Some people like to add a lot of spices and other flavorings, but I don't think that's necessary. Make sure your meat is fully submerged in the brine, keep it in the refrigerator, and pat dry before grilling. I usually brine poultry pieces and pork chops for at least a couple hours and whole poultry and pork roasts for at least 4 hours. Most things can stand to brine for up to 24 hours. After that, they can take on a "cured" texture and flavor.

Don't stress if you don't have the time (or refrigerator space) to brine your meat. Salting meat before grilling—sprinkling a light, even coating of coarse salt in a single layer—is essentially "dry brining" and serves a similar purpose in a shorter amount of time. Dry brining is better than wet brining for beef, lamb, and pork ribs, but you should season everything before grilling. When possible, I like to let the meat sit for at least 30 minutes after salting and before grilling, but I always break my own rules. The beauty of high-heat live-fire cooking is that the meat cooks quickly and acquires amazing flavor and texture, whether brined or not.

It's really satisfying to make chicken stock on the grill. The pot can sit in a corner of the grill as long as the grill is fired up, and the stock will only get better with each hour. If you have the ingredients on hand, it's worth making a batch for the freezer anytime you're cooking on the grill. But my chicken stock isn't just a subtle soup base; it's a dark, meaty, sweet soup unto itself, and with the chicken shredded into it and a loaf of great bread on the side, it's a satisfying meal. It's a great thing to make for the next day if you know you won't have time to cook. The stock is rich enough to substitute for beef broth in recipes.

# Chicken Stock on the Grill

*Makes about 12 cups*

| | |
|---|---|
| 12 cups water | 4 carrots |
| 8 garlic cloves | 4 celery stalks |
| 2-inch piece fresh ginger, peeled and sliced | 2 unpeeled white or red onions, halved |
| 4 whole star anise | Salt, for seasoning |
| 4 bay leaves | Chopped parsley leaves and lemon wedges, for serving |
| 1 tablespoon black peppercorns | |
| One 4-pound chicken, cut into 8 pieces | |

Wipe the grill grates with oil to prevent sticking. Build a two-zone fire. Your high-heat zone should have embers 1 to 2 inches from the cooking surface, with occasional flames licking it. To create your medium-heat zone, nudge the embers 2 to 3 inches lower than that.

Fill a stockpot with the water, garlic, ginger, star anise, bay leaves, and peppercorns and place over medium heat. Place the chicken, carrots, celery, and onions over high heat and cook, turning occasionally, until well charred all over, about 15 minutes total. When each ingredient is done, add it to the pot (it's important that each ingredient be very well browned—almost burnt—before adding to the pot). Cook the stock for at least 3 hours, adding additional water if necessary to keep the meat and vegetables covered. Season with salt at the end.

Remove the pot from heat. Remove the chicken pieces and shred the meat, discarding the skin and bones. Strain the stock, discarding solids.

To serve, place a pile of shredded chicken into each bowl and cover with hot stock. Pass the parsley and lemon wedges separately. The stock can be stored in a covered container in the refrigerator for up to 1 week or in the freezer for up to 6 months.

# Leftover Chicken Curry Salad

Serves 4

If you think of it, the next time you're grilling chicken, grill one or two extra. Cold grilled chicken is great on its own and even better in a salad like this one. It's also, of course, perfect for a picnic. Some weekends, I'll get up early and do all my grilling in the morning for an afternoon picnic. Add the Crudités with Grilled Green Goddess Dip (page 46), Eggplant Dip with Smoked Dates (page 67), Beets with Pickled Beet Greens (page 51), or even one of my ceviches (pages 113 and 116) and you can take the flavors of the outdoor kitchen anywhere. This salad is good on its own with grilled bread, but if you want to make sandwiches for a picnic, pack the bread separately so the sandwiches don't get soggy.

If you don't have leftover chicken, it's worth grilling one just for this salad. Grill one whole butterflied chicken, using the technique for Butterflied Chicken with Toasted Mustard Seed Oil (page 130), let cool to room temperature, then pick the meat from the bones.

1½ cups plain Greek-style yogurt

Juice of 2 lemons (about 6 tablespoons)

1 teaspoon ground turmeric

1 teaspoon ground cumin

½ teaspoon ground cinnamon

¼ teaspoon ground cardamom

1 teaspoon salt, plus more for seasoning

1 teaspoon pepper

1 tablespoon honey

4 cups grilled chicken, diced into ½-inch pieces or coarsely shredded

½ cup toasted walnuts, chopped

¼ cup dried currants

1 apple, of any variety, peeled, cored, and diced into ¼-inch pieces

3 celery stalks, finely chopped

1 jalapeño chile, stemmed, charred on the grill, or raw, minced

¼ cup each chopped fresh cilantro, basil, and mint (or any combination of the three)

In a large bowl, whisk together the yogurt, lemon juice, turmeric, cumin, cinnamon, cardamom, salt, pepper, and honey. Add the chicken and toss to coat. If preparing ahead of time, the chicken mixture can be stored in a covered container in the refrigerator for up to 2 days.

When ready to serve (or pack for a picnic), mix in the walnuts, currants, apple, celery, jalapeño, and herbs. Season with salt.

I'm a fan of using the same ingredients in multiple parts of a dish so I don't have to buy extra things at the store that are used once and then sit in my fridge forever. In this recipe, pineapple makes a fantastic marinade—pineapple has an enzyme called bromelain that tenderizes meat—and it's also used in a salsa to serve with the cooked chicken. The marinade caramelizes on the grill to create a tasty crust; baste the chicken with extra marinade as it grills.

Chicken breast sizes can vary wildly in stores, but I find that organic, free-range chicken breasts usually clock in at the reasonable size called for here. If yours are larger, just trim them to a sensible serving size.

To make the marinade: Slice the pineapple crosswise into 1-inch-thick rounds. Using a paring knife, remove the core from each round (this can be done roughly, since the core is edible). Chop half the pineapple coarsely; set aside the remaining half for the relish. Add the chopped pineapple to a blender, together with the jalapeño, onion, vinegar, garlic, and salt and blend until smooth. Transfer the marinade to a bowl, add the chicken breasts, and refrigerate, covered, for at least 8 hours or up to 24 hours.

Wipe the grill grates with oil to prevent sticking. Build a two-zone fire. Your high-heat zone should have embers 1 to 2 inches from the cooking surface, with occasional flames licking it. To create your medium-heat zone, nudge the embers 2 to 3 inches lower than that.

To make the relish: Toss the remaining pineapple in oil, honey, and salt to coat. Grill over medium heat until it is nicely caramelized, about 3 minutes per side. Meanwhile, grill the jalapeño and onion over medium heat until lightly charred, turning often, about 3 minutes for the jalapeño and 8 minutes for the onion. As they finish cooking, transfer the pineapple, jalapeño, and onion to a cutting board.

continued

# Marinated Chicken Breasts with Grilled Pineapple Relish

Serves 4

### Marinade

1 ripe pineapple, peeled but left whole

1 jalapeño chile

½ red onion

½ cup vinegar

1 tablespoon roasted garlic (see page 106)

1 tablespoon salt

4 boneless, skin-on chicken breasts, 6 to 8 ounces each

### Grilled Pineapple Relish

½ peeled pineapple (remaining from marinade prep)

Oil, for coating

Honey, for coating and seasoning, plus 1 tablespoon

Salt, for coating and seasoning

1 jalapeño chile

½ red onion, peeled and halved

¼ cup vinegar, plus more to taste

½ cup packed cilantro leaves, chopped

## Marinated Chicken Breasts with Grilled Pineapple Relish

continued

When they are cool enough to handle, coarsely chop the pineapple, jalapeño, and onion and add to a bowl with the vinegar, 1 tablespoon honey, and cilantro. Season with more salt, and add more vinegar or honey, if needed. Set aside until ready to serve.

Remove the chicken breasts from the marinade, shaking off any excess, and bring to room temperature. Place skin side down over high heat. After about 90 seconds, using tongs, rotate 45 degrees and cook for another 2 minutes. Flip the breasts and do the same on the other side. Once you have nice grill marks on both sides, move to medium heat and cook, turning often, until an instant-read meat thermometer, placed in the thickest part of a breast, reads 160°F on a meat thermometer. Transfer to a cutting board and let the breasts rest for 10 minutes before slicing and serving with the relish.

Most of my recipes that use pickled mustard seeds just use a little for tang and their caviarlike "pop." That's not the case here, where the mustard seeds are the star, used both in the marinade and the sauce. With just a few ingredients but manifold spicy-sour-sweet flavors, it's a dish equally suited to a weekday dinner and a special occasion.

# Butterflied Chicken with Pickled Mustard Seeds

Serves 4 to 6

Wipe the grill grates with oil to prevent sticking. Build a high-heat fire. Your high-heat zone should have embers 1 to 2 inches from the cooking surface, with occasional flames licking it.

To prepare each chicken, using kitchen shears, cut along both sides of the backbone and remove (your butcher can also do this for you). Place the chicken skin side up on the cutting board and apply firm pressure to the breastbone to flatten.

Add 1 cup of the mustard seeds to a blender together with the vinegar, 1 tablespoon of the honey, and the salt, and blend until smooth. Toss the chicken with the marinade and refrigerate, covered, for at least 2 hours or up to overnight. Remove the chicken from the marinade, wiping off any excess, and discard the marinade.

Grill the chickens, bone side down, over high heat for about 10 minutes. Flip the chickens, move to medium heat, and cook for another 30 minutes, or until an instant-read meat thermometer placed in the thickest part of the thigh reads 165°F. You can flip the chickens occasionally while cooking to give even color. During the last 5 minutes of cooking, brush them with honey. Transfer to a cutting board and let the chickens rest for 10 minutes before carving into serving pieces.

While the chickens are cooking, add the remaining 1 cup mustard seeds and the remaining 2 tablespoons honey to the blender and blend until smooth. Add additional honey and/or salt, if needed. To serve, smear the mustard seed puree on a large platter (or on 4 individual plates) and top with the chicken.

**Two 3- to 4-pound whole chickens**

**2 cups Pickled Mustard Seeds (page 154)**

**¼ cup vinegar**

**3 tablespoons honey, plus more for basting and*to taste**

**2 teaspoons salt, plus more for seasoning**

# Chicken Legs with Onion and Smoked Date Jam

Serves 4

Dark-meat chicken is your friend on the grill, because it's much harder to overcook than breasts. It can also take a more intense sauce. Most onion "jams" involve slowly sautéing the onions until caramelized, often with a lot of extra sweetener and added vinegar to try and balance it out. The result can be cloying, like bad Chinese American sweet-and-sour sauce. By quickly charring the onion before simmering with sugar and vinegar, you get a similar effect with more of a true onion flavor. The smoked dates add further depth.

4 skin-on chicken legs, including thighs

Salt, for coating

Onion and Smoked Date Jam

2 unpeeled red onions, halved

Oil, honey, and salt, for coating

6 pitted dates, smoked (see page 20)

½ cup sugar

1 cup vinegar

1 cup water

Wipe the grill grates with oil to prevent sticking. Build a medium-heat fire. Your medium-heat zone should have embers 3 to 5 inches from the cooking surface.

Rub the chicken legs with a light coating of salt and let them sit at room temperature for 30 minutes (see page 131). (You can also refrigerate the chicken legs for up to 24 hours, but bring them to room temperature and wipe off the salt before grilling.)

To make the jam: Toss the onions in oil, honey, and salt to coat. Grill, cut side down, over medium heat until well charred, about 5 minutes. Transfer to a plate, set aside until cool enough to handle, then peel and thinly slice and add to a saucepan. Coarsely chop the dates and add to the saucepan along with the sugar, vinegar, and water. Place over medium heat and simmer until reduced and deeply caramelized, about 45 minutes.

While the jam reduces, grill the chicken legs over medium heat, turning every 5 minutes or so, until the skin is dark brown or until an instant-read meat thermometer placed in the thickest part of the thigh reads 180°F (chicken legs and thighs are more tender when cooked to a higher temperature than chicken breasts). This should take 30 to 40 minutes total. Transfer to a cutting board and let rest for 10 minutes before cutting the thighs from the drumsticks. Serve immediately with the jam.

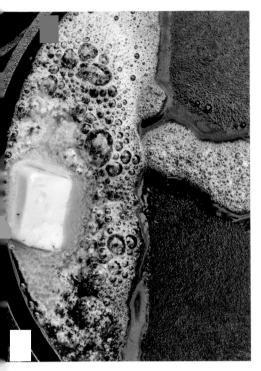

# Quail Salad with Roasted Plum Glaze and Candied Pine Nuts

Serves 4

I love cooking quail, and I don't know why it's not more popular in the United States. Maybe it's because it's always served as a dainty whole quail arranged on a plate with a dab of sauce. To me, quail is one of the most informal things to make: it cooks quickly, has great flavor, and it begs to be eaten with your hands. I wanted to play up the informality here by chopping the quail after cooking and throwing it into a salad. Eat the salad with one hand while you gnaw on the quail with the other.

The sweet plum glaze works great against the slightly bitter broccoli rabe. If you can't find broccoli rabe (or if it's too bitter for your taste), try making this with radicchio or black kale. You don't have to caramelize the pine nuts, but it makes a big difference, and once you pull off this pine nut brittle on the grill, you'll be candy-ing nuts for everything. I like doing quick candied nuts on the grill to serve guests as a snack while everything else is still cooking.

### Candied Pine Nuts

1 cup sugar

1 cup pine nuts

### Roasted Plum Glaze

6 large ripe plums

½ cup honey

½ cup vinegar

Salt, for seasoning

1½ pounds broccoli rabe

Oil and salt, for coating

Four 4- to 5-ounce semi-boneless quail, with backbone removed

Pomegranate seeds, for garnish

Wipe the grill grates with oil to prevent sticking. Build a two-zone fire. Your high-heat zone should have embers 1 to 2 inches from the cooking surface, with occasional flames licking it. To create your medium-heat zone, nudge the embers 2 to 3 inches lower than that.

To make the candied pine nuts: Line a baking sheet with parchment paper. Place the sugar in a small cast-iron skillet over medium heat and slowly melt it, swirling the pan often (remove from the heat if it starts to burn). Remove the pan from the heat, stir in the pine nuts, and immediately pour onto the baking sheet in as thin a layer as possible. Use toothpicks to separate the nuts as best as you can (you can also wait for them to harden, then break or cut them into small pieces). Set aside.

To make the glaze: Roast the plums directly in the embers until mushy. Remove from the embers with tongs and brush off the ash. Squeeze the flesh from the skins into

continued

## Quail Salad with Roasted Plum Glaze and Candied Pine Nuts

continued

a bowl, discarding the skins and pits. Mash the plum pulp with the honey and vinegar, and season with salt. Set aside.

Toss the broccoli rabe with the oil and salt and place over medium heat. Cook until tender and lightly charred, about 5 minutes, then transfer to a cutting board and coarsely chop. Set aside.

Press the quail flat and coat with the plum glaze, reserving at least 2 tablespoons of glaze. Grill over high heat for about 3 minutes per side (check one with a knife at its meatiest spot; the juices should run clear even if the meat is still pink). Transfer to a cutting board and roughly chop each quail into quarters.

To serve, in a large bowl, toss the broccoli rabe with the remaining 2 tablespoons plum glaze, plus more as needed. Add the quail, pine nuts, and pomegranate seeds, and serve immediately.

Here, we'll dry brine the duck in a light coating of salt and let it sit for an hour. Duck responds well to brining since it can dry out on the grill. This also helps the skin crisp up. As the duck skin cooks, a lot of fat drips into the fire. I like to nestle halved onions, fennel, endive, or radicchio directly in the embers, cut side up, to catch the duck drippings as they cook.

Even people I know who don't like fresh papaya love this jam. You can also make the jam with mango, persimmon, kiwi, or peach and serve it with chicken or pork.

Wipe the grill grates with oil to prevent sticking. Build a medium-heat fire. Your medium-heat zone should have embers 3 to 5 inches from the cooking surface.

To make the jam: Add the papaya to a saucepan together with the habanero, vinegar, sugar, and salt. Cook over medium heat until the mixture is syrupy, about 30 minutes. The jam can be made up to 4 days in advance and stored in a tightly covered container in the refrigerator; reheat before serving.

Score the duck skin in a crosshatch pattern and rub all over with the salt. Let the duck sit at room temperature for about an hour (see page 131), then wipe off any excess salt before grilling (sometimes a lot of salt can get between the crosshatching). (You can also refrigerate the duck for up to 6 hours before grilling.)

Grill the duck breasts over medium heat, skin side down, until the skin is dark brown and crisp, about 10 minutes. Flip and cook until medium-rare, about 5 minutes more. Transfer to a cutting board and let rest for 5 minutes before slicing across the grain into serving pieces. Serve with the jam.

# Duck Breasts with Spicy Papaya Jam

Serves 4

**Spicy Papaya Jam**

1 papaya, peeled, seeded, and coarsely chopped

1 habanero, stemmed, seeded, and minced (use gloves or a paper towel when handling habaneros)

2 cups vinegar

½ cup sugar

1 teaspoon salt

Four 6-ounce boneless, skin-on duck breasts

Salt, for coating

# Pork

# Grilled Pork Chops with Peanut–Honey Mustard Sauce

Serves 4

I've always liked honey mustard, and it's always in my fridge at home, since I have a kid who also loves it. I was thinking about how to make it more "adult," and nothing was making sense. So I started thinking of other flavors I had loved as a kid—kind of like, "if you can't beat 'em, join 'em"—and peanut butter came to mind. Any sweet or spicy sauce goes well with grilled pork, and here the vinegar and mustard seeds offset the richness of both the pork and the peanuts. A friend told me that this reminded him of Thai peanut sauce, but it just reminds me of my childhood.

I like a rustic sauce, and I usually just blend peanuts in a food processor until they get peanut-buttery. Natural-style peanut butter works just as well or even a regular smooth peanut butter if you don't like the texture of the natural kind.

**Peanut–Honey
Mustard Sauce**

1 cup natural-style
peanut butter

¼ cup vinegar

2 tablespoons honey

2 tablespoons Pickled
Mustard Seeds
(page 154)

1 teaspoon ground
turmeric or 1 small
knob fresh turmeric,
peeled

2 garlic cloves, minced

Salt, for seasoning

Four 12- to 16-ounce
bone-in pork rib chops,
1½ inches thick

Salt, for coating

Wipe the grill grates with oil to prevent sticking. Build a two-zone fire. Your high-heat zone should have embers 1 to 2 inches from the cooking surface, with occasional flames licking it. To create your medium-heat zone, nudge the embers 2 to 3 inches lower than that.

To make the sauce: Combine the peanut butter, vinegar, honey, mustard seeds, turmeric, and garlic in a food processor. Puree until smooth, then season with salt. Set aside. The sauce can be made in advance and stored, covered, in the refrigerator for up to 2 weeks.

Score the fatty edge of each pork chop by cutting shallow crosshatched slices into it; this helps keep it from curling up as it cooks. Salt the chops well and let them sit for 30 minutes (see page 131). Place over high heat for about 3 minutes per side to get deep grill marks. Using tongs, sear the fatty edges until the fat browns and crisps. Move to medium heat and grill, turning occasionally, for about 10 minutes more, until an instant-read meat thermometer placed in the thickest part of a chop reads 145°F. Transfer to a serving dish and let the pork rest for 10 minutes before serving with the peanut sauce.

# MUSTARD SEEDS TWO WAYS

Mustard has been used with grilled foods around the world for ages, and mustard seeds are even more versatile than prepared mustard, whose pungency isn't always welcome. Mustard seeds have an earthiness that feels natural with grilled food, while their sharpness has a cleansing effect, refreshing your mouth between bites. I most often use them in these two preparations.

## Pickled Mustard Seeds

Makes about ½ cup

**These seeds can be used whole or pulsed to a coarse puree in a food processor with salt and honey to taste. I put them in almost any salad or sandwich or on top of grilled meat.**

Combine 2 tablespoons each of yellow and brown mustard seeds (or use all yellow), ½ cup cider vinegar, and 1 tablespoon honey in a small saucepan over medium heat and simmer for 30 minutes, stirring often (add water if the liquid evaporates). Cool to room temperature and store, covered, in the refrigerator for up to 3 months.

## Toasted Mustard Seed Oil

Makes about 2 cups

**I find myself often using this oil in place of regular oil for basting meat and vegetables as they grill or as the oil in salad dressings and dips. Someone always asks what the elusive flavor is.**

Using a mortar and pestle or a rolling pin, crack ⅓ cup yellow mustard seeds so they break apart without turning to powder. Add the seeds to a small saucepan with 2 cups oil and heat to a simmer over low heat; the seeds should gently sizzle without turning color or the oil burning. After 5 minutes, let cool and strain through a fine-mesh strainer or cheesecloth. Mustard seed oil will keep, covered, in the refrigerator for at least 3 months.

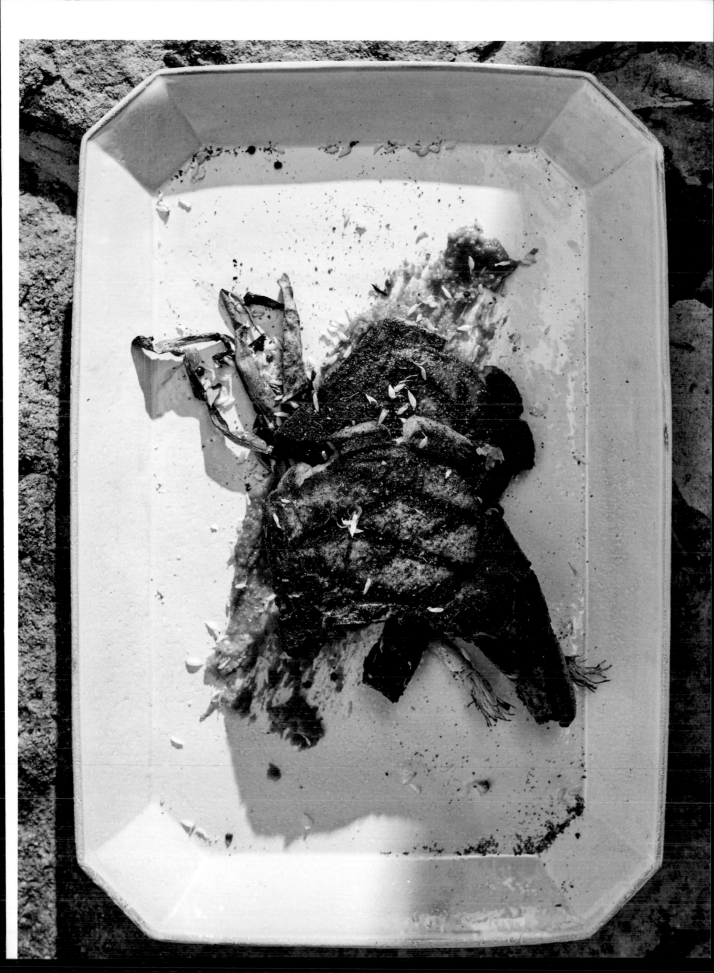

I usually use pork chops that are at least 1½ inches thick, but I like slightly thinner ones for this quick recipe. The glaze reminds me a little of the marinade for the thin-cut pork chops you get in Vietnamese restaurants. Like my fermented pineapple sauce (see page 112), this honey vinegar is a great introduction to fermentation. Give it a try!

To make the honey vinegar: Combine the honey and water in a quart jar, cover with a cloth (this will let air in but will keep fruit flies out), and secure with a rubber band. Keep in a warm place—a high shelf or a countertop that receives direct sunlight—for at least 4 weeks, or until fermented and slightly effervescent. Strain through a fine-mesh strainer or cheesecloth and store in a sealed jar in the refrigerator.

Wipe the grill grates with oil to prevent sticking. Build a high-heat fire. Your high-heat zone should have embers 1 to 2 inches from the cooking surface, with occasional flames licking it.

Salt the chops well and let them sit for 30 minutes (see page 131). Coat a cast-iron pan with oil and place over high heat. When the oil starts to smoke, add the pork chops and cook for 2 minutes per side, until deeply browned. Remove the chops to a plate. Deglaze the pan with the honey vinegar and reduce for about 45 seconds, then return the pork chops to the pan. Continue reducing the honey vinegar and baste the pork with it, until it reduces to the consistency of maple syrup. Let the pork chops rest for 5 minutes before serving.

# Cast-Iron Pork Chops with Honey Vinegar

Serves 4; makes 2 cups of honey vinegar

**Honey Vinegar**
¼ cup honey
2 cups warm water

Salt and oil, for coating
Four 8- to 12-ounce bone-in pork rib chops, 1 inch thick

# Hartwood Spiced Spareribs

Serves 4 to 6

One of my sharpest food memories from childhood is of the spareribs at the Chinese restaurant that my uncle would always take me to. They were fall-apart tender, with this sticky-sweet sauce that was also just spicy and smoky enough to keep me thinking about them as an adult. Eventually I got obsessed with trying to re-create them in a way that made sense for my adult taste buds, and I came up with this recipe. The spice mix is kind of a Mexicanized version of Chinese five-spice powder that balances perfectly with the sweet-tart sauce, which has the bite of habanero chiles.

Spareribs are typically cooked "low and slow" on the grill, but in Mexico, I've seen plenty of people just throw them directly over a fire, and they come out just fine. My technique isn't that low, but the aluminum foil wrapping keeps the juices intact and helps the ribs slowly break down. Just move them to a cooler part of the grill if you suspect they're cooking too "high and fast."

### Spice Mix

½ cup whole allspice berries

⅓ cup coriander seeds

⅓ cup black peppercorns

4 ancho chiles, stemmed and seeded

10 chiles de árbol, stemmed and seeded

2 tablespoons ground cinnamon

1 teaspoon ground cloves

2 full racks of pork spareribs (6 to 8 pounds)

Salt, for coating

### Sauce

1 white or red onion, quartered

5 large tomatoes

2 habanero chiles, stemmed and seeded (use gloves or a paper towel when handling habaneros)

1 cup pineapple juice

½ cup vinegar

¼ cup honey

¼ cup roasted garlic (see page 106)

Wipe the grill grates with oil to prevent sticking. Build a two-zone fire. Your high-heat zone should have embers 1 to 2 inches from the cooking surface, with occasional flames licking it. To create your medium-heat zone, nudge the embers 2 to 3 inches lower than that.

To make the spice mix: Toast the allspice, coriander, and peppercorns in a cast-iron pan over medium heat until fragrant, about 5 minutes; set aside. Add the chiles to the same pan and toast just until fragrant but not charred, 1 to 2 minutes. Blend all of the ingredients to a coarse powder in a blender or food processor or in batches in a spice grinder. The spice mix can be stored in a covered container in the refrigerator for up to 1 week but is best used the same day.

Coat the ribs liberally with salt and ¼ cup of the spice mix. Grill over high heat until the ribs are charred and smoky, about 5 minutes per side. Remove and wrap tightly in aluminum foil. Place over medium heat and cook for

continued

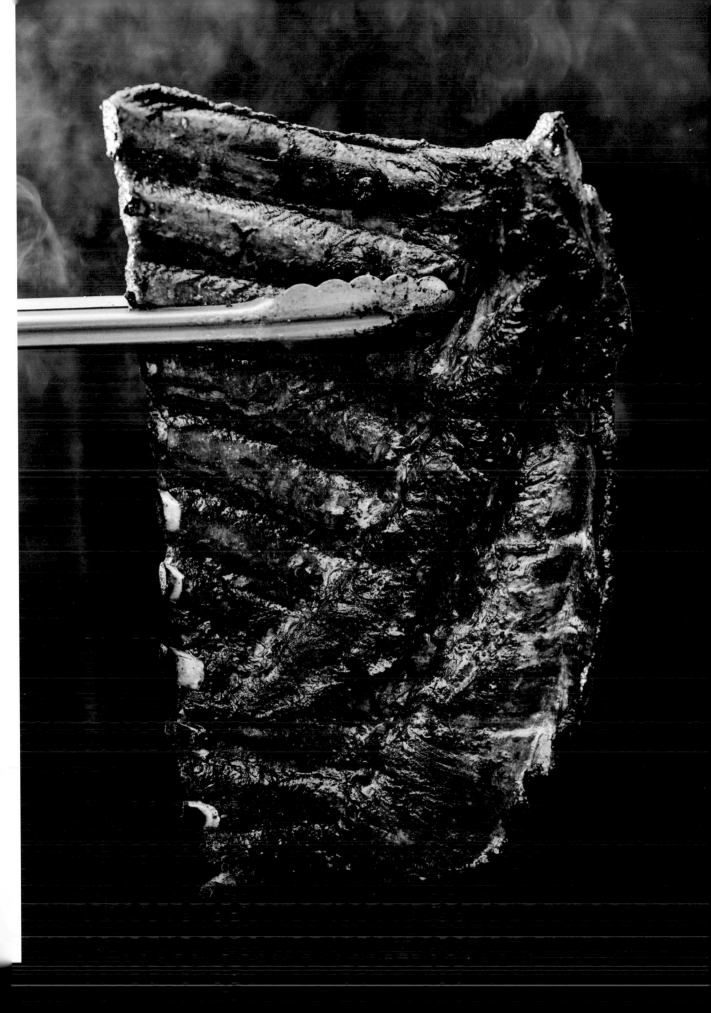

## Hartwood Spiced Spareribs
continued

at least 2 hours (check after 2 hours; they're done when you can pull the ribs apart with your fingers or tongs).

To make the sauce: While the ribs are cooking, grill the onion, tomatoes, and habaneros over medium heat, turning occasionally, until charred all over, 10 to 15 minutes. Transfer with tongs to a saucepan and add the pineapple juice, vinegar, honey, garlic, and 2 tablespoons of the spice mix. Simmer over medium heat for 1 hour, or until the tomatoes break down and the whole thing starts to look like spaghetti sauce. Transfer to a blender and blend until smooth; set aside.

When the ribs are done, transfer to a plate and remove the foil. Brush them generously with some of the sauce, and grill over high heat until charred, about 2 minutes per side. Remove the ribs from the grill and tear into irregular pieces of two or three ribs each. Pile on a platter and serve. Pass the remaining sauce separately.

This is a riff on *tacos al pastor*, where chile-rubbed pork is piled onto tacos with pineapple and onion. I combined some of the key pastor flavors in this jam, which became a staple for "family meal" at Hartwood, usually with steak tacos, and a staple for me at home. Doing it with a whole pork roast makes it perfect for a group. You can let the jam simmer away on a corner of the grill while you cook the pork roast, or you can just make the jam in advance—it keeps in the fridge for up to 2 weeks and is great with almost any simply grilled meat from this book.

Wipe the grill grates with oil to prevent sticking. Build a two-zone fire. Your high-heat zone should have embers 1 to 2 inches from the cooking surface, with occasional flames licking it. To create your medium-heat zone, nudge the embers 2 to 3 inches lower than that.

To make the jam: Dice the pineapples into small pieces (about ¼ inch), including the cores, and add to a large stockpot with the onions, chiles, sugar, vinegar, and salt. Place over medium heat and let the mixture simmer, stirring occasionally but more often toward the end of cooking, until the mixture reduces and becomes sticky and jamlike, 45 minutes to 1 hour. Season with more salt and sugar, if needed. The jam can be stored in a covered container in the refrigerator for up to 2 weeks; bring to room temperature before serving.

Rub salt all over the pork roast and let it sit, uncovered, in the fridge for at least 4 hours and up to 24 hours (see page 131). Remove the roast from the fridge an hour before you start grilling. Place it over high heat and brown all sides of the meat, 5 to 10 minutes per side. Move to medium heat and cook, turning occasionally, until an instant-read meat thermometer, placed in the thickest part of the roast, reads 145°F (start checking the temperature after 45 minutes). Transfer to a cutting board and let the roast rest for 20 minutes before slicing into serving pieces. Serve with the jam.

# Pork Loin with Pineapple, Red Onion, and Chile de Árbol Jam

Serves 8

### Chile de Árbol Jam

2 ripe pineapples, peeled but left whole

2 red onions, peeled, quartered, and thinly sliced

8 chiles de árbol

2 cups sugar, plus more if needed

4 cups vinegar

1 tablespoon salt, plus more if needed

Salt, for coating

1 boneless pork loin roast (about 3 pounds)

# Kielbasa with Jalapeño Relish

Serves 4

Kielbasa is a gift for the grill, since in the United States, the sausages are usually smoked and precooked, so you just need to heat them through. The relish here is just a quick pickle of charred jalapeños, so I'm not sure why it's so good, but I use it on everything: eggs, tacos, roast chicken, and grilled veggies. It reminds me of a spicier, sharper hot dog relish, so it's a natural for hot dogs and especially hearty smoked sausages like kielbasa.

### Jalapeño Relish

12 jalapeño chiles, stemmed, halved lengthwise, and seeded

Oil, for coating

1 cup vinegar

1 tablespoon honey

2 teaspoons salt

1½ pounds kielbasa, cut into 5-inch lengths

Wipe the grill grates with oil to prevent sticking. Build a medium-heat fire. Your medium-heat zone should have embers 3 to 5 inches from the cooking surface.

To make the relish: Toss the jalapeños with the oil, place over medium heat, and grill until charred, about 2 minutes per side. Using tongs, transfer the jalapeños to a bowl, then tightly cover with plastic wrap to allow them to steam in their own heat for 15 minutes.

Meanwhile, mix together the vinegar, honey, and salt in a bowl until the salt dissolves. Mince the jalapeños and combine with the vinegar mixture. The relish can be stored in a covered container in the refrigerator for at least 2 weeks; cover it with a thin layer of oil to ensure freshness.

To cook the kielbasa, place over medium heat and grill, turning often, until it is charred and hot throughout, about 10 minutes. Serve immediately with the relish.

This is my take on *poc chuc*, a Yucatecan dish of pork marinated in sour orange and quickly grilled. It's kind of a deconstructed schnitzel, except that it's not fried.

Fatty pork shoulder is usually slow-cooked for shredding, but when it's cut and pounded thin, it grills up tender and juicy—even juicier when it's quickly brined. If the steaks from the butcher are more than ½ inch thick, cut them "book style" before pounding: slice them horizontally almost all the way through, then open as if you're opening a book. Use a meat pounder or rolling pin to pound evenly to a ¼-inch thickness.

Wipe the grill grates with oil to prevent sticking. Build a high-heat fire. Your high-heat zone should have embers 1 to 2 inches from the cooking surface, with occasional flames licking it.

To make the marinade: Mix together the water, lime juice, garlic, sugar, salt, and peppercorns in a large bowl and let sit until the sugar and salt dissolve.

Add the pork to the marinade and let sit at room temperature for 1 hour or refrigerate, covered, for up to 4 hours. Just before grilling, remove the pork from the marinade and pat dry.

Grill the pork over high heat for 1 minute, then rotate 45 degrees and cook for another minute. Flip and repeat on the other side. Transfer to a serving platter in a high pile, sprinkle with salt, and serve with lemon wedges.

# Pork Paillards in a Pile

Serves 4 to 6

### Marinade

4 cups water

Juice of 2 limes
(about ¼ cup)

4 garlic cloves, minced

¼ cup sugar

2 tablespoons salt

2 teaspoons black
peppercorns, cracked

2 pounds thin-cut
boneless pork shoulder
steaks, ¼ inch thick

Salt, for finishing

Lemon or lime wedges,
for serving

This is a classic hearty soup that couldn't be easier to make. Sometimes, when I have the grill fired up for something else, I make a pot to have a ready-made dinner for a busy day in the coming week (it will keep for up to 5 days in the fridge and gets better as it sits). You don't need to grill the ham hocks, but if you have the time for it, it adds a lot of depth of flavor. The daikon radish helps tenderize the beans and adds a subtle peppery note, but it can be omitted.

# Bean and Ham Hock Soup

*Serves 4 to 6*

Wipe the grill grates with oil to prevent sticking. Build a two-zone fire. Your high-heat zone should have embers 1 to 2 inches from the cooking surface, with occasional flames licking it. To create your medium-heat zone, nudge the embers 2 to 3 inches lower than that.

Grill the ham hocks over high heat until deeply browned, 5 to 10 minutes per side.

While the ham hocks are cooking, coat a stockpot or Dutch oven with oil and place over medium heat. Add the onion, carrots, and celery and sauté until the onions start to brown, about 10 minutes. Add the ham hocks, beans, radish (if using), bay leaves, cumin, and water. Cook for at least 2 hours over medium heat, until the beans are very soft (they should crush easily between your fingers), adding more water if necessary to keep the beans covered. If the soup seems too thin, simmer, uncovered, to thicken, or, if it's too thick, add more water until you achieve the desired consistency.

Remove the ham hocks (and the daikon, if using) and, when the ham is cool enough to handle, pick the meat from the bones, discarding the bones and skin. Return the meat to the pot and season with salt. Serve immediately.

1½ pounds smoked ham hocks

Oil, for coating

1 white onion, minced

2 carrots, minced

2 celery stalks, minced

1 pound dried black beans

3-inch-long piece daikon radish (optional)

4 bay leaves

1 tablespoon cumin seeds, crushed or ground

10 cups water, plus more if needed

Salt, for seasoning

# Baby Back Ribs with Tamarind Barbecue Sauce

Serves 4

Unlike spareribs, baby back ribs don't need to be cooked all day over low heat; as long as they're cooked through, they're good to go.

This is the barbecue sauce you should always have in your fridge. It's delicious with any pork dish, a meaty grilled fish, or simply served on top of a burger for an added kick. It's also great stirred into stewed beans or brushed on roasted sweet potatoes.

Buy tamarind paste, not the pulp that is sold in hard blocks (tamarind paste is the pulp with the seeds and fibers removed). You'll find it at Southeast Asian and Mexican groceries, larger supermarkets, or online.

### Tamarind Barbecue Sauce

1 tablespoon oil

1 white onion, peeled and thinly sliced

½ cup chipotle chiles, stemmed and seeded

1 cup freshly squeezed orange juice (from 4 to 6 oranges)

1 cup tamarind paste

8 garlic cloves, chopped

1 cup vinegar, plus more if needed

1 cup water, plus more if needed

2 tablespoons honey, plus more if needed

1 teaspoon salt, plus more if needed

4 pounds baby back ribs (ask your butcher to remove the membrane)

Salt and pepper, for seasoning

Wipe the grill grates with oil to prevent sticking. Build a two-zone fire. Your high-heat zone should have embers 1 to 2 inches from the cooking surface, with occasional flames licking it. To create your medium-heat zone, nudge the embers 2 to 3 inches lower than that.

To make the sauce: Heat the oil in a medium saucepan over high heat. Add the onion and cook until softened and slightly caramelized, about 5 minutes. Add the chipotles and cook for another 2 minutes. Deglaze the pan with the orange juice, add the tamarind paste, garlic, vinegar, water, honey, and salt, and simmer for 20 minutes or until the liquid thickens enough to coat a spoon. Cool slightly, then transfer to a blender and blend until very smooth, adding more vinegar and/or water if needed to thin to a consistency of tomato sauce. Add more vinegar, honey, or salt, if needed. The sauce can be stored in a covered container in the refrigerator for up to 2 weeks.

Season the ribs with salt and pepper. Grill over medium heat, turning often, for about 45 minutes or until they're no longer pink in the middle and the meat starts to shrink away from the bones at the edges. Baste frequently with the sauce so it builds up a thick, tacky crust. Transfer to a cutting board and immediately slice the ribs into two-rib portions. Serve the ribs on a platter.

# Beef & Lamb

## Anatomy of a Rub

I cringe when I see recipes for meat rubs—or, worse, expensive store-bought rubs—that are nothing more than powdered spices. A good rub is so easy to make: salt, freshly ground spices, and a little moisture so it sticks to the meat. For sweetness, I like honey, which has a more savory texture than sugar and also acts as a glue. One of my favorite "rubs," especially for pork, is just a thin rub of honey, maybe with some roasted garlic, then a coating of salt and pepper.

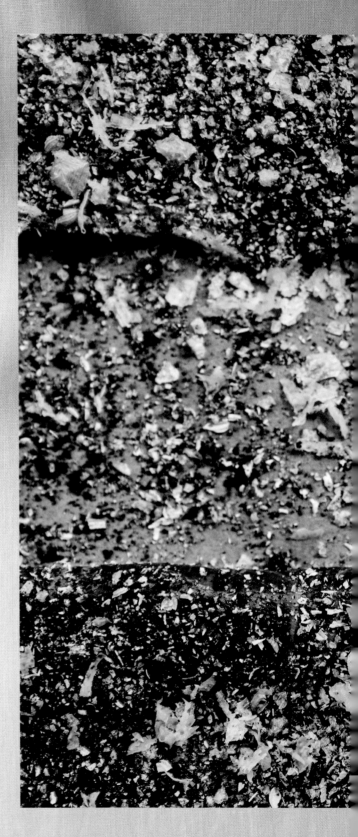

# Skirt Steak with Coriander-Ancho Rub and Gribiche

*Serves 4 to 6; makes about 1 cup of gribiche*

For the longest time, I couldn't figure out why I liked the smell of coriander seeds so much. Yes, coriander smells like flowers and citrus and curry powder. It also smells exactly like Froot Loops. It's usually used in Indian spice mixtures, but I wanted to see how it would stand on its own. This rub combining coriander with the sweetness and gentle heat of ancho chiles tastes incredibly complex, given how simple it is. It's one I make a lot, especially with lamb and beef.

Everyone loves skirt steak. It's affordable, has a rich beefy flavor and lots of fat marbling, and stays tender and juicy when cooked fast over high heat. As the rub sits on the steak, the moisture from the meat starts to rehydrate the chiles, creating a fantastic crust when it hits the grill.

### Coriander-Ancho Rub

2 tablespoons coriander seeds

4 ancho chiles, stemmed, seeded, and roughly torn

2 teaspoons salt

1 tablespoon honey

### Gribiche

4 hard-boiled eggs, peeled and minced

2 tablespoons minced parsley leaves

2 tablespoons minced shallots

Zest and juice of 1 lemon (about 3 tablespoons juice)

½ cup oil

Salt and pepper, for seasoning

2 pounds skirt steak (ask your butcher for "outside skirt")

Wipe the grill grates with oil to prevent sticking. Build a two-zone fire. Your high-heat zone should have embers 1 to 2 inches from the cooking surface, with occasional flames licking it. To create your medium-heat zone, nudge the embers 2 to 3 inches lower than that.

To make the rub: Place the coriander and chiles in a skillet over medium heat and stir until toasted and fragrant but not burnt, 3 to 5 minutes. Cool slightly and blend to a fine powder in a blender or food processor. Mix with the salt and honey. The rub will keep tightly covered in the refrigerator for up to 2 weeks.

To make the gribiche: Combine the eggs, parsley, shallots, and lemon zest and juice in a bowl. Slowly add the oil, while whisking constantly. Season with salt and pepper. Gribiche can be covered and refrigerated for up to 8 hours, but should be served on the day it's made.

Coat the steaks liberally with the rub. Let them rest uncovered in the refrigerator for at least 1 hour and up to 4 hours. Place the steak over high heat for about 90 seconds, then turn 45 degrees and cook for another 90 seconds. Flip and repeat on the other side, for a total of 6 minutes. Move to medium heat and test for doneness by slicing into one steak; you don't want it cooked beyond medium-rare. Transfer steak to a cutting board and let rest for 5 minutes, then slice against the grain and serve with the gribiche.

# Standing Rib Roast with Ember-Baked Potatoes

Serves 6 to 8

This is a showstopper, and roasts that are larger than 5 pounds can be cooked in exactly the same way, making them perfect for a holiday dinner. Don't be intimidated by cooking a substantial and expensive piece of meat on the grill. As long as you have a meat thermometer, you can't go wrong. I find it really relaxing to hang around the grill over a large piece of meat, turning it occasionally and rubbing it with herbs, shallots, apples, or whatever else is lying around. The "herb broom" is fun to use, and it ends up in the sauce. The potatoes roast while the meat cooks, and the sauce comes together in a couple minutes, making this the best kind of holiday centerpiece: one that lets you spend time with friends and family instead of being stuck in the kitchen all day.

Black garlic is made by gently heating garlic for several weeks, until its sharp components break down via the Maillard reaction (the same process behind searing steak and roasting coffee beans) into a sweet black paste. Black garlic is packaged and sold in specialty stores and online. This recipe is a good excuse to familiarize yourself with it; there's no substitute for its sweet and funky flavor. Here it's whipped into sour cream for a kind of savory mousse.

One 4- to 5-pound standing rib roast

Salt and pepper, for seasoning

1 apple, of any variety

2 large shallots

1 large bunch mixed herbs (with stems), such as rosemary, sage, tarragon, and parsley, tied at the base to make a "broom"

6 to 8 large russet potatoes (at least 1 per person)

¼ cup store-bought black garlic, peeled

2 cups sour cream

Season the roast generously with salt and pepper and let it sit, covered, at room temperature for 2 hours before cooking. This will bring the meat to room temperature all the way through, so you don't risk having cool meat at the center after cooking.

Meanwhile, wipe the grill grates with oil to prevent sticking. Build a medium-heat fire. Your medium-heat zone should have embers 3 to 5 inches from the cooking surface.

Place the roast bone side down over medium heat and put the apple and shallots directly in the embers. After about 30 minutes, start turning the roast occasionally, so that every exposed part gets deeply browned (the bone side

continued

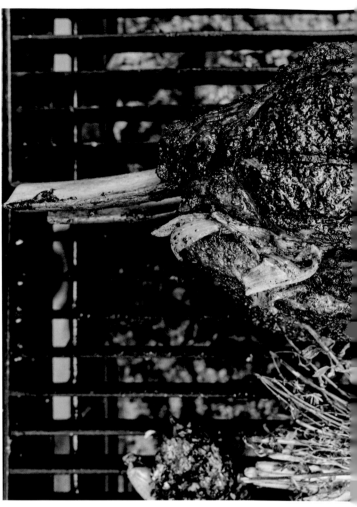

## Standing Rib Roast with Ember-Baked Potatoes

### continued

should get the most time on the grill, since that meat takes longer to cook).

As the roast browns and the fat renders from the surface, brush the roast firmly with the herb broom, allowing some of the leaves to fall onto the roast and into the fire (let the herbs sit on the grill when you're not using them). When the shallot and apple are very soft and almost falling apart, use tongs to rub them all over the roast as it cooks. You want to build up a shallot-apple-herb crust that will both flavor and protect the meat.

After about 1 hour, put the potatoes in the embers under the roast so they catch some of the drippings. No need to prick the potatoes; if any of them explode, which is unlikely, it makes a good story, and they'll absorb more of the tasty beef fat. The roast should take about 2 hours to cook through (move it to higher heat if it's not building up a deeply colored crust), but after about 90 minutes, start checking the temperature with an instant-read meat thermometer. Cook to an internal temperature of 130°F (because of its ample fat marbling, rib roast is best when it's not too rare).

Remove the roast to a cutting board using potholder-covered hands or two large forks. Tent with aluminum foil and let it rest for 20 to 30 minutes. When the potatoes can be easily pierced with a butter knife, use tongs to remove them, wrap with foil, and let sit on a corner of the grill to keep warm.

While the roast is resting, mash the black garlic with a fork in a bowl until very smooth. Add the sour cream and whisk until smooth and fluffy. Using scissors, snip the herbs from the herb broom directly into the sauce.

Remove the potatoes from the foil and arrange them around the roast on the platter. To serve, carve the roast at the table and pass the sauce alongside.

Mole can be intimidating to the American home cook, due to the many hard-to-find ingredients, labor-intensive techniques, and endless hours of simmering. I wanted to come up with an "American" mole with readily available ingredients and a weekday-friendly cooking time. This is a fresh, sweet, and spicy mole with a deep butterscotch color and smooth texture and all of the complexity of a great Mexican mole.

I pair this American mole with a great American cut of beef, the tri-tip (aka Newport steak), which is cut from the bottom sirloin and is lean and tender but with full beefy flavor. Its silky texture makes it a natural with mole.

# Tri-tip with American Mole

Serves 4 to 6

Wipe the grill grates with oil to prevent sticking. Build a two-zone fire. Your high-heat zone should have embers 1 to 2 inches from the cooking surface, with occasional flames licking it. To create your medium-heat zone, nudge the embers 2 to 3 inches lower than that.

To make the mole: Place all of the chiles in a large bowl with hot water to cover and soak for 30 minutes. Drain and return to the bowl.

Grill the apple, banana, and onion over medium heat, turning occasionally, until they are charred and soft, about 5, 7, and 10 minutes, respectively. Peel the banana and place it in a bowl together with the apple, onion, garlic, peppercorns, cinnamon, coriander, cloves, cardamom, walnuts, and vinegar. Working in two batches, transfer the contents of the bowl to a blender and puree until very smooth, adding just enough stock to keep the blades turning. Season with salt and/or sugar. Transfer the mixture to a large skillet or saucepan and cook over medium heat for 15 minutes, until it's the consistency of tomato sauce (if too much liquid evaporates, add more stock).

continued

## American Mole

8 pasilla chiles, stemmed and seeded

8 ancho chiles, stemmed and seeded

1 apple, of any variety, halved and cored

1 banana, unpeeled

1 white or red onion, halved

1 head roasted garlic (page 106)

1 teaspoon black peppercorns

1 teaspoon ground cinnamon

1 teaspoon coriander seeds

½ teaspoon ground cloves

¼ teaspoon ground cardamom

½ cup toasted walnuts

¼ cup vinegar

Chicken or beef stock, as needed

Salt and sugar, for seasoning

2 pounds beef tri-tip steaks

Salt and pepper, for coating

## Tri-tip with American Mole

## continued

If the tri-tip steaks are of varying thicknesses, pound them with your fists so they're a little more uniform. Coat them generously with salt and pepper and let them sit for 20 to 30 minutes. Place the steaks over high heat and sear for about 5 minutes per side, until they are deeply browned. Move them to medium heat and cook, turning often, until an instant-read meat thermometer, placed in the thickest part of one steak, reads 125°F. Transfer to a cutting board and let the steaks sit for 15 minutes before slicing against the grain. Serve with warm mole.

# Filet Mignon
# with Herb Mayo

Serves 4

You don't see filet mignon much anymore in cookbooks, which is a shame, because it has a beautiful flavor and texture, although it can be a little challenging to cook. You want to develop a nice crust on it without losing any juices, since it doesn't have a lot of juice to spare. I like starting it on the plancha in lots of butter, then finishing it over the fire.

A simple herb mayo won't overwhelm the meat, and since you're already spending a lot on the meat, there's no need to add expensive frills. And even if you're a rare steak lover, cook filet mignon at least to medium-rare, since its subtle flavor comes out with more cooking.

For an extra-smoky touch, burn the fennel fronds and fresh herbs on the grill before mincing them.

Four 8-ounce filet mignon steaks, 2 inches thick

Salt and pepper, for coating

½ cup (1 stick) butter

**Herb Mayo**

½ cup minced mixed fresh herbs, such as parsley, basil, and mint

2 tablespoons minced fennel fronds (may substitute minced tarragon leaves)

1 teaspoon lemon zest

1 cup mayonnaise

Salt, for seasoning

Wipe the grill grates with oil to prevent sticking. Build a two-zone fire. Your high-heat zone should have embers 1 to 2 inches from the cooking surface, with occasional flames licking it. To create your medium-heat zone, nudge the embers 2 to 3 inches lower than that.

Coat the steaks generously with salt and pepper. Heat a plancha or cast-iron griddle over high heat. Add the butter, and when it starts to smell nutty and turn color, add the steaks and turn them in the butter to coat. Sear on all sides until a dark crust forms, 2 to 3 minutes per side. Transfer to the grill over medium heat and let cook, turning often, until an instant-read meat thermometer, placed in the thickest part of one steak, reads 125°F. Transfer to a platter and let the steaks rest for 10 minutes before serving.

While the meat is cooking, make the mayo: In a small bowl, mix the herbs, fennel, and lemon zest into the mayonnaise and season with salt. Serve the steaks with the mayo on the side.

Grilling for one is a huge luxury. It's you with a fire and zero responsibilities—no worrying about what time dinner has to be on the table or how entertained your guests are. Rib eye steaks are incredibly delicious, hard to overcook due to the ample fat marbling throughout the meat, and look "complete" on the plate, as opposed to some cuts that beg for sauces and side dishes. Roast the onion while the embers heat, then finish the onions while the steak grills. Open a bottle of the best red wine you can get your hands on.

Wipe the grill grates with oil to prevent sticking. Build a two-zone fire. Your high-heat zone should have embers 1 to 2 inches from the cooking surface, with occasional flames licking it. To create your medium-heat zone, nudge the embers 2 to 3 inches lower than that.

Roast the onion directly in the embers until it feels soft when prodded with tongs, about 20 minutes. Transfer to a cutting board, remove skin, and chop the flesh finely. Coat a small cast-iron pan with oil and place over medium heat. Add the onion and cook until it's deep brown. Add the molasses and cook for another 5 minutes, then add the butter, season with salt, and keep the sauce warm on a corner of the grill while you cook the rib eye.

Coat the steak generously with salt and pepper and let sit for 20 to 30 minutes. Place over high heat and sear for about 6 minutes per side, turning often, until it's deeply browned. Remove from heat when an instant-read meat thermometer, placed in the thickest part, reads 130°F. Transfer to a serving plate and let sit for 10 minutes before eating with the caramelized onions.

# Rib Eye for One with Caramelized Onions

Serves 1

1 unpeeled white or red onion

Oil, for coating

1 tablespoon molasses (may substitute honey)

1 tablespoon butter

Salt, for seasoning and coating

One 1-pound bone-in rib eye steak, about 1½ inches thick

Pepper, for coating

# Smoked Short Ribs with Chile Glaze

*Serves 4 to 6*

This may be my favorite meat recipe in this book, simply because nothing makes me happier than having the grill fired up all day: I'm like an Italian grandma making a Sunday sauce. I sometimes use the time to make other stuff on the grill to use later, like Bean and Ham Hock Soup (page 165), Chicken Stock on the Grill (page 135), mole sauces, or grilled pickles. To break up the cooking time, smoke the ribs one day and braise them the next. The smoked ribs will keep in the fridge for 3 days.

**Rub**

3 chipotle chiles, toasted, stemmed, and seeded

3 pasilla chiles, toasted, stemmed, and seeded

1 tablespoon salt

1 tablespoon fennel seeds, ground

1 tablespoon sugar

1 tablespoon honey

1 tablespoon roasted garlic (see page 106)

5 pounds bone-in beef short ribs

Salt, for seasoning

2 white onions, coarsely chopped

2 carrots, coarsely chopped

3 celery stalks, coarsely chopped

Celery Root and Horseradish Slaw (page 55), for serving

Prepare the smoker and bring to between 220° and 240°F (see page 20). To make the rub: Grind the chiles to a powder in a blender or spice grinder, then transfer to a bowl together with the salt, fennel, sugar, honey, and garlic (the mixture should resemble wet sand). The rub can be made ahead, covered, and refrigerated for up to 1 week.

Score the tops of the short ribs, season liberally with salt, and then coat with the rub. Pack any extra rub on top of the short ribs and place the ribs, meat side up, directly on a shelf in the smoker. Smoke for 6 hours.

Wipe the grill grates with oil to prevent sticking. Build a two-zone fire. Your high-heat zone should have embers 1 to 2 inches from the cooking surface, with occasional flames licking it. To create your medium-heat zone, nudge the embers 2 to 3 inches lower than that.

Using tongs, transfer the ribs to a Dutch oven and add the onions, carrots, celery, and enough water to cover three-quarters of the ribs. Cover tightly and place on the grill over medium heat for 3 hours. Remove the ribs and set aside. Strain the broth through a medium-mesh strainer, discarding the vegetables, and skim the fat from the surface. Return the broth to the pot and bring to a boil over high heat. Reduce by about half and then return the ribs to the pan. Continue reducing the sauce, while turning the ribs occasionally, until the sauce becomes a glaze for the ribs. Remove the bones from the ribs, transfer the ribs and sauce to a serving platter, and serve immediately, with the slaw on the side.

# Dry-Aged Shell Steak with Whipped Blue Cheese

Serves 4

Dry-aging beef removes moisture from the meat, leaving a beefier flavor and, interestingly, a more tender texture. Ask your butcher for beef that's been dry-aged about 45 days. It should smell like buttered popcorn, a quality that is accentuated on the grill, and it should never be cooked beyond medium-rare. This steak tastes incredible with the sweet funkiness of the blue cheese, but also works great with a bright green chimichurri butter.

To make a green chimichurri butter (pictured on page vii), blanch ½ cup each cilantro, basil, oregano, and parsley leaves. Transfer to an ice bath, then dry between paper towels. Add the dried, blanched herbs, 2 garlic cloves, 1 grilled poblano (see page 52; stem and seeds removed), and the finely grated zest and juice of 1 lime to a food processor. While the processor is running, slowly add ½ cup olive oil. Blend until completely smooth. Add ½ pound, cubed and softened unsalted butter to the food processor and blend until smooth. Season with salt. The butter can be stored in a covered container in the refrigerator for up to 5 days.

One 24-ounce dry-aged New York strip steak

Salt and pepper, for coating

½ cup blue cheese, such as Roquefort, Gorgonzola, Bleu d'Auvergne, or Danish Blue

2 tablespoons oil

Wipe the grill grates with oil to prevent sticking. Build a two-zone fire. Your high-heat zone should have embers 1 to 2 inches from the cooking surface, with occasional flames licking it. To create your medium-heat zone, nudge the embers 2 to 3 inches lower than that.

Pat the steak dry and coat with salt and pepper. Let sit for 20 to 30 minutes. Place the steak over high heat for 5 minutes, then flip and repeat. Move to medium heat and cook for another 2 to 3 minutes, until an instant-read meat thermometer, placed in the thickest part of the steak, reads 125°F. Transfer to a cutting board and let rest for 10 minutes.

While the steak is cooling, combine the cheese and oil in a food processor and blend until smooth and fluffy, about 1 minute. Slice the steak against the grain and top with the blue cheese mixture just before serving.

This dish is a great showcase for my butcher's salt. When I have a perfect piece of meat, I often grill it without any other rub. Porterhouses are two steaks in one: New York strip on one side and tenderloin filet on the other. They're always crowd-pleasers.

Wipe the grill grates with oil to prevent sticking. Build a high-heat fire. Your high-heat zone should have embers 1 to 2 inches from the cooking surface, with occasional flames licking it.

Pat the steaks dry and coat with the salt. Let sit for 20 to 30 minutes. Place the steaks over high heat. Cook until grill marks are deeply seared into the meat, about 2 minutes, then turn the steaks 45 degrees and cook for another 2 minutes. Flip and repeat on the other side. Cook, flipping occasionally, until an instant-read meat thermometer, placed in the thickest part of one steak, reads 125°F (this shouldn't take much longer than 8 to 10 minutes total). Transfer to a cutting board and let rest for 10 minutes before slicing and serving.

# Porterhouse Steak with Butcher's Salt

Serves 4

2 porterhouse steaks, about 1½ inches thick

Butcher's salt (see page 36), for coating

# Split Marrow Bones with Hearts of Palm

*Serves 8 as an appetizer*

Marrow bones are an impressive sight on the grill, and crisp lemon-flecked veggies help cut their intense richness. If you can't find fresh hearts of palm (some specialty markets and online sources have them), use endives—canned hearts of palm aren't worth grilling.

4 beef marrow bones, split lengthwise (ask your butcher to do this for you)

Oil, for coating

Salt, for seasoning

1 pound fresh hearts of palm or endives

1 lemon, quartered

Toasted bread, for serving

Wipe the grill grates with oil to prevent sticking. Build a two-zone fire. Your high-heat zone should have embers 1 to 2 inches from the cooking surface, with occasional flames licking it. To create your medium-heat zone, nudge the embers 2 to 3 inches lower than that.

Keep the marrow bones in the refrigerator until you are ready to cook. Just before cooking, brush the marrow (cut) sides with the oil and sprinkle with salt. Place cut side down over high heat and cook just until the bones start to char, about 90 seconds. Watch the bones closely and flip them over if the marrow starts to melt and drip into the fire. Turn the bones and cook, cut side up, until the marrow starts to bubble around the edges or becomes hot to the touch. Keep warm on the side of the grill until you're ready to serve.

While the bones are cooking, cut the hearts of palm in half lengthwise, rub with oil, and grill over medium heat until charred and tender, 6 to 8 minutes per side (about 3 minutes per side if using endives). Transfer to a cutting board and coarsely slice.

Transfer the marrow bones to a platter and sprinkle with more salt. Pile the hearts of palm around them and squeeze the lemon over them. Serve immediately with bread and with your smallest forks and spoons to get every bit of marrow out.

# New York Strip with Poblano Worcestershire Sauce

Serves 4 to 6

Worcestershire sauce is a great marinade for steak, but I wanted to make a version from scratch, with my own spin on the classic condiment. My sauce is somewhere between a roasted chile salsa and traditional Worcestershire sauce. It screams to be served on steak, but you could also try it in a Bloody Mary or in a salad dressing.

New York strip is a tender boneless cut with lots of tasty fat marbling; it's a little like rib eye but not quite as rich. Strip steak is the large part of a T-bone steak.

**Poblano Worcestershire Sauce**

3 poblano chiles

2 white or red unpeeled onions, halved

Oil and salt, for coating

3 tablespoons vinegar

2 tablespoons soy sauce

1 tablespoon freshly squeezed lime juice

1 tablespoon roasted garlic (see page 106)

1 tablespoon honey

2 pounds New York strip steak

Wipe the grill grates with oil to prevent sticking. Build a high-heat fire. Your high-heat zone should have embers 1 to 2 inches from the cooking surface, with occasional flames licking it.

To make the sauce: Toss the poblanos and onions in oil and salt. Grill over high heat, turning occasionally, until they are completely blackened, about 10 minutes for the poblanos and a little longer for the onions. Transfer with tongs to a bowl, then tightly cover with plastic wrap to allow them to steam in their own heat and to cool enough to handle. Peel the skin from the chiles with your fingers, but don't worry if some burnt bits remain. Remove and discard the stems and seeds. Cut the peel and root end from the onions.

Place the chiles and onions in a blender together with the vinegar, soy sauce, lime juice, garlic, and honey and blend until completely smooth. The sauce can be stored in a covered container in the refrigerator for up to 2 weeks.

Coat the steaks generously with the sauce and let them marinate for 1 hour. Place the steaks over high heat and grill about 5 minutes per side, until an instant-read meat thermometer, placed in the thickest part of one steak, reads 125°F. Use tongs to sear the edges of the meat as well. Transfer to a cutting board and let rest for 10 minutes. Slice against the grain and serve, passing additional sauce at the table.

I prefer cooking lamb chops individually, rather than grilling an entire rack of lamb, so that each side gets contact with the grill. This bright sauce is more like a glaze than a thick and rich barbecue sauce. It's amazing with lamb, but its gently sweet tart-smoky flavor works with almost any meat, fish, or vegetable, such as Pork Paillards (page 163), Chicken Legs (page 142), or Cauliflower Steaks (page 45). Rather than using it as a condiment, baste your food with the sauce as it cooks: the flavors will concentrate, and it will add an appealing sheen.

# Lamb Chops with Tomatillo Barbecue Sauce

Serves 4

Wipe the grill grates with oil to prevent sticking. Build a two-zone fire. Your high-heat zone should have embers 1 to 2 inches from the cooking surface, with occasional flames licking it. To create your medium-heat zone, nudge the embers 2 to 3 inches lower than that.

To make the sauce: Place the tomatillos and jalapeños over medium heat, turning occasionally, until slightly charred all over, about 8 minutes total. Transfer to a plate and cut the tomatillos in half, reserving the juice. Halve the jalapeños lengthwise, remove the stems, and scrape out some of the seeds and veins. Combine the tomatillos (with their juice) and jalapeños together with the vinegar, water, sugar, and salt in a medium saucepan and simmer over low heat for 20 to 30 minutes, until the sauce is reduced and slightly syrupy. Cool the mixture slightly, transfer to a blender, and blend until very smooth. The sauce can be covered and refrigerated for up to 1 week.

Salt the chops well, then place them over high heat and sear on all sides (use tongs to crisp up the fat on the edges), about 2 minutes per side. Move to medium heat and cook, turning often, until just past medium-rare (about 135°F on an instant-read meat thermometer), about 5 minutes more in total. Transfer to a serving platter and let rest for 5 minutes before serving, passing the sauce separately.

**Tomatillo Barbecue Sauce**

10 large tomatillos, peeled and rinsed

5 jalapeño chiles

2 cups vinegar

2 cups water

¾ cup sugar

1 tablespoon salt

2½ pounds lamb ribs or loin chops, each at least 1 inch thick

Salt, for seasoning

Tender rib chops—the ones with the "handle"—are cute, but I love lamb loin chops, aka lamb T-bones. They have a hearty texture and flavor and a wraparound fat cap that crisps up beautifully on the grill.

I'd like to see people use more chamomile in food; it has a floral, apple-y flavor that goes with a lot of things. It also doesn't lose much flavor when it's dried: if you can't find chamomile as a loose herb (check a health food store or online), you could just empty out a teabag, as long as it's 100 percent chamomile. Bee pollen is a fun garnish to use with honey, but it's totally optional.

Wipe the grill grates with oil to prevent sticking. Build a two-zone fire. Your high-heat zone should have embers 1 to 2 inches from the cooking surface, with occasional flames licking it. To create your medium-heat zone, nudge the embers 2 to 3 inches lower than that.

To make the chutney: Coat a sauté pan with oil and place over medium heat. Add the onion and cook until tender, about 5 minutes. Add the apricots, chamomile, star anise, cardamom, honey, and water. Cook until almost all of the liquid has cooked off and the mixture is thick and syrupy. (The mixture can be made to this stage up to 5 days in advance and refrigerated in a covered container.) Discard the star anise. Stir in the mint, almonds, and lemon juice.

Score the fatty edge of each lamb chop by cutting shallow crosshatched slices into it.

Salt the chops well, then place them over high heat and sear on all sides (use tongs to crisp up the fat on the edges), about 2 minutes per side. Move to medium heat and cook, turning often, until just past medium-rare (about 135°F on an instant-read meat thermometer), about 5 minutes more in total. Transfer to a serving platter and drizzle with honey, sprinkle with chamomile, and serve with warm chutney alongside.

# Lamb T-Bones with Apricot-Chamomile Chutney

Serves 4

### Apricot-Chamomile Chutney

Oil, for coating

1 white or red onion, chopped

1 cup dried apricots, chopped

1 tablespoon dried chamomile, plus more for garnish

2 whole star anise

3 green or white cardamom pods, with seeds removed

¼ cup honey, plus more for garnish

1 cup water

2 tablespoons chopped mint leaves

2 tablespoons chopped toasted unsalted almonds

Juice of 1 lemon (about 3 tablespoons)

2½ pounds lamb loin chops, at least 1 inch thick

Salt, for seasoning

Summer squash, aka zucchini, is one of the easiest vegetables to grow in a home garden (and one of the cheapest to buy at a farmers' market). This salad was the result of having too much squash and not wanting to bake zucchini bread. It's a good side dish with almost anything, but it transforms these burgers. Small, young zucchini are delicious raw, but frying half of them adds a ton of depth of flavor and texture. Serve extra squash salad as a side dish.

These can be traditional burgers, open-faced or sliders for a party, or Greek-style bun-less patties. Feta and yogurt are naturals with lamb, but if you're not a lamb fan, the sauce will still work with any ground meat.

Wipe the grill grates with oil to prevent sticking. Build a two-zone fire. Your high-heat zone should have embers 1 to 2 inches from the cooking surface, with occasional flames licking it. To create your medium-heat zone, nudge the embers 2 to 3 inches lower than that.

To make the salad: Pour oil into a small sauté pan to a depth of ¼ inch. Place over high heat until the oil ripples. Add half of the zucchini and fry until golden brown. Remove with a slotted spoon and place on a plate lined with paper towels. When it has cooled, add the fried zucchini to a bowl with the remaining raw zucchini, radishes, and jalapeños. In a small bowl, whisk the lemon juice and 6 tablespoons oil with the pepper and salt and add to the salad, tossing to coat. Sprinkle the cilantro on top.

To make the sauce: In a small bowl, mix the feta and yogurt with a fork until smooth. Add the garlic, lemon juice and zest, fennel, parsley, and pepper. The sauce can be stored in a covered container in the refrigerator for up to 3 days.

To make the burgers: Coat the small sauté pan with oil. Place over high heat and add the onion and garlic. Cook

continued

# Lamb Burgers with Summer Squash Salad and Feta-Yogurt Sauce

Serves 4

### Summer Squash Salad

Oil, for frying, plus 6 tablespoons

2 pounds summer squash, thinly sliced

8 radishes, sliced paper-thin

4 jalapeño chiles, stemmed, seeded, and minced

Juice of 1 lemon (about 3 tablespoons)

6 tablespoons oil

1 teaspoon pepper

½ teaspoon salt

2 tablespoons minced cilantro leaves

### Feta-Yogurt Sauce

½ cup crumbled feta cheese

½ cup plain whole-milk yogurt

1 garlic clove, minced

Juice and zest of ½ lemon

1 tablespoon minced fennel fronds (may substitute minced tarragon leaves)

1 tablespoon minced parsley leaves

1 teaspoon pepper

### Lamb Burgers

Oil, for coating

½ red onion, minced

2 garlic cloves, minced

1 pound ground lamb

2 tablespoons chopped fennel fronds (may substitute chopped tarragon leaves)

2 tablespoons chopped parsley leaves

1 teaspoon ground cumin

1 teaspoon celery seed

¼ teaspoon ground cinnamon

Salt, for seasoning

4 hamburger buns, toasted

### Lamb Burgers with Summer Squash Salad and Feta-Yogurt Sauce

### continued

until they soften and start to brown, then transfer to a bowl. When the onion and garlic are no longer hot to the touch, add the lamb, fennel, parsley, cumin, celery seed, and cinnamon and mix well with your hands. Divide the mixture into four patties.

Salt the burgers just before grilling. Grill over high heat for 1½ to 2 minutes per side to get good grill marks. Move to medium heat and cook to the desired doneness, 2 to 4 minutes more per side (the cooking time will vary with burger thickness).

To serve, place the burgers on the buns and top with the sauce and the salad, passing extra sauce and salad at the table.

# Desserts

# Pumpkin-Pasilla
# Ice Cream

*Makes about 1 quart*

One 3- to 4-pound
pie pumpkin or
butternut squash

3 pasilla chiles,
stemmed and seeded

2½ cups heavy cream

1 cup whole milk

½ vanilla bean,
split lengthwise

¼ teaspoon salt

6 egg yolks

¾ cup sugar

Dried chiles and winter squash go really well together. Each are sweet and earthy, and, when combined, they bring out the deeper and more complex flavors in the other. Grilled winter squash with mole is a great example of this, as are tacos of roast winter squash with a red chile salsa. It might seem odd to combine these two savory ingredients for dessert, but they make a deeply flavored ice cream that is especially festive in the winter months.

Build a two-zone fire. Your high-heat zone should have embers 1 to 2 inches from the cooking surface, with occasional flames licking it. To create your medium-heat zone, nudge the embers 2 to 3 inches lower than that.

Place the pumpkin directly in the embers and cook until the skin collapses and a butter knife passes easily through it, about 20 minutes. Remove to a cutting board with tongs (have a large spoon ready for support if the pumpkin collapses), let rest until cool enough to handle, then cut in half and remove the seeds. Scoop the flesh out with a spoon (discard the skin and stem), and mash with a fork. Measure 1 cup and reserve the remainder.

Toast the chiles in a pan over high heat just until aromatic, about 60 seconds on each side. Grind to a coarse powder in a coffee grinder or blender. Measure 3 tablespoons and discard the remainder.

In a medium saucepan, combine the chile powder, cream, milk, vanilla bean, and salt. Let it sit for 30 minutes in the fridge. While the mixture steeps, whisk the egg yolks and sugar in a bowl until the sugar dissolves and the mixture is pale and fluffy.

Remove the saucepan from the fridge and place over medium heat. Heat just until the mixture begins to simmer (it should be hot to the touch, with bubbles starting to form around the perimeter) and remove from the heat.

Whisk about ½ cup of the cream mixture into the egg yolk mixture, then whisk the yolk mixture back into the saucepan. Place the pan back over medium heat and whisk constantly, until the mixture thickens enough to

coat the back of a wooden spoon (this should take 3 to 5 minutes). Remove from the heat and whisk in the pumpkin puree.

Strain the mixture through a fine-mesh strainer into a bowl, discarding any solids. Cover and refrigerate until very cold, at least 2 hours and up to 2 days. (If you want a stronger pumpkin flavor, add up to ½ cup more of the reserved pumpkin puree.)

Process the mixture in an ice cream maker according to the manufacturer's directions, then transfer to an airtight container and freeze until ready to serve. The ice cream will keep in the freezer for up to 2 weeks.

Bay leaf has a very subtle flavor that's best highlighted without any competing herbs or spices. Dried bay leaves lose their potency very quickly once the package or jar is opened, so, for this recipe, be sure your bay leaves haven't been in an opened package for months. Dried bay leaves also freeze well in airtight plastic freezer bags. This recipe is inspired by a similar pudding that my good friend Scott Ehrlich used to make when we worked together.

# Bay Leaf Pudding

Serves 6

Build a medium-heat fire. Your medium-heat zone should have embers 3 to 5 inches from the cooking surface.

Combine the whole milk, cream, condensed milk, and bay leaves in a medium-size heavy pot and place over medium heat. Bring to a simmer (little bubbles should appear around the edges; move to a hotter part of the grill if not). Let simmer for 15 minutes, then remove the bay leaves.

While the milk mixture heats, whisk the egg yolks and sugar in a large bowl for at least 2 minutes, until the sugar dissolves and the mixture turns pale. Very slowly add about half of the milk mixture, whisking constantly, then return that mixture to the pot.

Whisk the pudding over medium heat until it thickens enough to thickly coat a spoon. Pour into serving dishes and chill for at least 4 hours and up to 3 days (cover with plastic wrap after 4 hours). When ready to serve, top with the chopped almonds and salt.

3 cups whole milk

2 cups heavy cream

¾ cup sweetened condensed milk

8 bay leaves

5 egg yolks

1 cup sugar

½ cup toasted unsalted almonds, coarsely chopped

Pinch of salt

# Burnt Strawberry
# Ice Cream

Makes about 1 quart

1 pint strawberries,
stemmed and quartered

5 egg yolks

1 cup sugar

¼ teaspoon salt

2 cups heavy cream

1 cup whole milk

Ripe fruit is important here because the sugars caramelize on the grill, but if your strawberries are underripe, toss them with a little honey before grilling. Charring the berries amps up their flavor and adds a subtle bitter note that stops the ice cream from being too sweet and one-dimensional.

This recipe works with almost any fruit: instead of the strawberries, try 4 grilled large bananas, 8 plums, 4 peaches, or even 2 cups of coarsely pureed corn kernels (see page 65).

Build a medium-heat fire. Your medium-heat zone should have embers 3 to 5 inches from the cooking surface.

Put the strawberries in a single layer in a cast-iron skillet and place the skillet directly in the embers. Cook, without stirring, until the bottoms of the strawberries start to burn; this should take 6 to 8 minutes. Transfer to a bowl and mash the strawberries well with a fork.

Whisk the egg yolks, sugar, and salt in a bowl until the sugar dissolves and the mixture becomes pale and fluffy. Combine the cream and milk in a medium saucepan and place over medium heat. Heat just to a simmer (it should be hot to the touch, with bubbles starting to form around the perimeter) and remove from the heat.

Whisk about ½ cup of the cream mixture into the egg yolk mixture, then whisk the yolk mixture back into the saucepan. Place the pan back over medium heat and whisk constantly, until the mixture thickens enough to coat the back of a wooden spoon (3 to 5 minutes). Remove from the heat and whisk in the strawberry puree.

Strain the mixture through a fine-mesh strainer or cheesecloth into a bowl, discarding any solids. Cover and refrigerate until very cold, at least 2 hours and up to 2 days.

Process the mixture in an ice cream maker according to the manufacturer's directions, then transfer to an airtight container and freeze until ready to serve. The ice cream will keep in the freezer for up to 2 weeks.

Grilled fruit is such an easy and refreshing dessert, especially after a heavy meal. You can use any firm fruit here; tropical fruits are usually recommended for grilling, but apples, pears, and melons work well, too. Your embers stay hot while you eat, so just throw the fruit on the grill when you want dessert. Use an interesting honey and garnish with any herbs or nuts you have lying around.

# Grilled Fruit with Yogurt and Honey

Serves 4

Wipe the grill grates with oil to prevent sticking. Build a medium-heat fire.

Cut the fruit into large pieces about 1 inch thick. Toss with the oil to coat. Place each piece over the hottest part of the grill and cook for about 2 minutes. Using tongs, rotate the fruit 90 degrees and continue cooking for another minute. Flip and repeat on the other side. You're not looking to "cook" the fruit so much as heat it through and give it nice grill marks. Brush the fruit lightly with the ¼ cup honey while grilling. Transfer to a serving platter or individual dishes and serve warm with a dollop of yogurt drizzled with honey.

2 pounds fruit, such as pineapples, melons, star fruits, plantains, mangos, apricot, figs, peaches, apples, or pears, peeled, seeded, or cored if necessary

Oil, for coating

¼ cup honey, for grilling, plus more for serving

1 cup plain Greek-style yogurt, for serving

# Black Peppercorn Panna Cotta with Stewed Plums

Serves 4

The unique flavor of black pepper really shines with creamy desserts. Panna cotta seems like an intimidating dish to make at home—let alone on the grill—but it's no more difficult than cooking any custard-based dessert on a stovetop. You can top the panna cotta with grilled fruit or just serve it on its own.

2¼ cups heavy cream

1 vanilla bean, split lengthwise

1 tablespoon black peppercorns, crushed

1 cup sugar

4 sheets gelatin

4 ripe plums, pitted and halved

Honey, oil, and salt, for coating

½ cup water

Wipe the grill grates with oil to prevent sticking. Build a medium-heat fire. Your medium-heat zone should have embers 3 to 5 inches from the cooking surface.

Pour the cream into a saucepan. Scrape the seeds from the vanilla bean into the cream along with the pod. Add the peppercorns and ½ cup of the sugar and place over medium heat. When it comes to a simmer, with small bubbles around the edges, move to a cooler part of the grill to steep for at least 5 minutes.

Meanwhile, "bloom" the gelatin sheets in a bowl of ice water for 2 minutes until softened. Lift the sheets from the water and squeeze gently to remove excess water. Add the gelatin to the infused cream and whisk to combine. Strain through a fine-mesh sieve or cheesecloth and divide among 4 large (6- to 8-ounce) ramekins. Cover with plastic wrap and refrigerate until set, at least 2 hours and up to 24 hours.

Toss the plums in honey, oil, and a pinch of salt and grill over medium heat until nicely charred, about 90 seconds per side. Using tongs, remove the plums and let cool. Slice the plums and place into a saucepan over medium heat with the remaining ½ cup sugar and the water. Cook until the liquid is syrupy, about 10 minutes. Let cool and then serve atop the cold panna cotta.

Smoking chocolate is easier than it sounds. Fat absorbs smoke very well, and 70% dark chocolate is about half cocoa butter. You can also, of course, make this without smoking the chocolate—the chipotle provides some inherent smokiness.

# Smoked Chocolate Mousse

Serves 4

| | |
|---|---|
| 8 ounces dark chocolate (70% cacao), coarsely chopped | 1 teaspoon ground cinnamon |
| 1 cup heavy cream | 1 teaspoon ground instant espresso |
| 3 eggs, separated | 1 teaspoon ground chipotle or smoked paprika |
| 1 teaspoon salt, plus more for the egg whites | 1 teaspoon vanilla extract |
| ¾ cup sugar | ½ cup (1 stick) butter |

Build a medium-heat fire. Your medium-heat zone should have embers 3 to 5 inches from the cooking surface.

To smoke the chocolate, place it in a small heatproof bowl. Put the bowl in a smoker (the smoker temperature should be very low, under 80°F) or set it inside a larger bowl and surround it with embers, cover tightly with plastic wrap or aluminum foil, and let sit for 1 hour.

Using a hand mixer on high speed, whisk the heavy cream until soft peaks form. Place the bowl over ice to keep cold. Rinse and dry the beaters.

In a separate bowl, combine the egg whites and a pinch of salt and mix on high speed for about 30 seconds. While the mixer is running, slowly add ½ cup of the sugar and mix until glossy, stiff peaks have formed. Set aside in a cool place. Rinse and dry the beaters again.

In a large bowl, combine the egg yolks, the remaining ¼ cup sugar, the cinnamon, espresso, chipotle, vanilla, and the 1 teaspoon salt. Mix on high speed until doubled in volume, about 3 minutes.

Combine the chocolate and butter in the top of a double boiler and place on the grill to melt over medium heat. Immediately stir in the egg yolk mixture until no streaks remain. Carefully fold in the egg white mixture, working in two batches, and then add the whipped cream in two batches, trying not to deflate the mixture too much. Divide the mousse among 4 large (6- to 8-ounce) ramekins and refrigerate until set, at least 1 hour and up to 24 hours. Serve chilled.

# Grilled Banana Trifle with Toasted Peanut Streusel

Serves 4

This dish reminds me of those banana puddings, layered with vanilla pudding and Nilla wafers, you would find at an old-school diner or your grandmother's house. The streusel and mascarpone cream can be made days in advance and stored in the fridge, so this can come together in minutes at the grill.

**Toasted Peanut Streusel**

1 cup (2 sticks) butter

1 cup all-purpose flour

½ cup granulated sugar

½ cup chopped salted peanuts

1 teaspoon ground cinnamon

1 teaspoon salt

1½ cups mascarpone

½ cup smooth peanut butter

3 tablespoons confectioners' sugar

2 tablespoons honey, plus more for coating

Whole milk, as needed

4 bananas

Oil, for coating

Wipe the grill grates with oil to prevent sticking. Build a medium-heat fire. Your medium-heat zone should have embers 3 to 5 inches from the cooking surface.

To make the streusel: Melt the butter in a large sauté pan over medium heat. Add the flour, granulated sugar, peanuts, cinnamon, and salt, and stir continuously until everything is toasted but not burnt, about 10 minutes. Set aside to cool.

In a bowl, whisk together the mascarpone, peanut butter, confectioners' sugar, honey, and just enough milk to give it the consistency of thick whipped cream.

Peel the bananas, slice each in half lengthwise, and toss with oil and honey to coat. Grill over medium heat until caramelized, about 2 minutes per side. Transfer to a plate or cutting board and cut each banana half into four pieces.

In a clear-sided trifle dish or in individual ramekins or jelly jars, layer the mascarpone mixture, the bananas, and the streusel; repeat so you end up with 6 layers total. Serve immediately.

This is a no-bake cheesecake, perfect for making ahead, so you only have to grill the grapes before serving. The roasted-grape garnish looks impressively rustic at the table.

Wipe the grill grates with oil to prevent sticking. Build a two-zone fire. Your high-heat zone should have embers 1 to 2 inches from the cooking surface, with occasional flames licking it. To create your medium-heat zone, nudge the embers 2 to 3 inches lower than that.

To make the crust: In a food processor, crush the graham crackers. Add the brown sugar and butter and blend until the mixture holds together when pinched between your fingers. Pat very firmly into the bottom of a 9-inch springform pan and refrigerate for at least 1 hour.

To make the filling: Using a hand mixer on high speed, beat the cream cheese and granulated sugar until the mixture is very fluffy and the sugar has dissolved, about 3 minutes. Beat in the sour cream, vanilla, and salt.

In another bowl, with the hand mixer on high, beat the cream with the cream of tartar until it forms stiff peaks. Fold into the cream cheese mixture. Pour the filling into the springform pan, cover with plastic wrap, and refrigerate for at least 6 hours or up to 5 days.

To make the syrup: In a heavy pot over high heat, combine the grapes, granulated sugar, and water and bring to a boil. Move to medium heat and cook for 10 minutes. Pour into a fine-mesh strainer or cheesecloth set over a bowl, pushing the grapes through with a rubber spatula and extracting as much juice as possible; discard the solids. Return the juice to the pot and add the pectin, lime zest and juice. Return to a boil over high heat and cook for 1 minute. (To test for the right texture, pour a tablespoon on a plate; it should be a thick, syrupy texture when it cools.) Set the pot aside to cool.

Roast the 2 bunches of grapes directly in the embers just until they start to pop and shrivel, about 2 minutes. Remove with tongs and brush off the ash. To serve, pour the syrup over the cheesecake, top with the grapes, slice, and serve.

# Concord Grape Cheesecake

Serves 8 to 12

### Crust

7 ounces graham crackers

¼ cup firmly packed dark brown sugar

½ cup (1 stick) butter, at room temperature

### Cream Cheese Filling

Three 8-ounce packages cream cheese, at room temperature

¾ cup granulated sugar

¼ cup sour cream

1 teaspoon vanilla extract

Pinch of salt

1½ cups heavy cream

¼ teaspoon cream of tartar

### Grape Syrup

2 cups stemmed Concord grapes, plus 2 whole bunches for garnish

¼ cup granulated sugar

¼ cup water

1 teaspoon powdered pectin

1 teaspoon lime zest

1 tablespoon freshly squeezed lime juice

# Cocktails

# Burnt Blood Orange and Bourbon Cocktail

*Makes 4*

4 blood oranges

¾ cup bourbon

1 tablespoon sugar, plus more for rimming the glasses

**Blood oranges have an intense flavor with undertones of raspberry and a slight bitterness. Giving them a smoky char makes them pair even better with bourbon.**

Wipe the grill grates with oil to prevent sticking. Build a high-heat fire. Your high-heat zone should have embers 1 to 2 inches from the cooking surface, with occasional flames licking it.

Cut 3 of the oranges in half and grill, cut side down, over high heat until charred. Halve the remaining orange, cut into thick slices, and grill until charred on both sides; set aside. Squeeze the orange halves to get 1 cup juice.

Add the juice, bourbon, and sugar to a cocktail shaker. Add ice to fill the shaker almost to the rim. Shake well for about 30 seconds to ensure the sugar dissolves and the drink is well chilled. Strain into sugar-rimmed coupe or martini glasses and garnish each with a charred orange slice.

# Rosemary-Gin Sour

*Makes 4*

8 sprigs of rosemary

Ice cubes

¾ cup gin

6 tablespoons freshly
squeezed lemon juice
(from 2 lemons)

¼ cup simple syrup

Lemon slices, plain
or grilled, for garnish
(optional)

Burnt—or even still flaming—herbs like rosemary, thyme, sage, and lavender make great cocktail garnishes. I love the way rosemary smoke merges with the botanicals in gin. To make the simple syrup, just mix 2 parts sugar to 1 part water, bring to a boil just to dissolve the sugar, then let cool.

Wipe the grill grates with oil to prevent sticking. Build a high-heat fire. Your high-heat zone should have embers 1 to 2 inches from the cooking surface, with occasional flames licking it.

Burn the rosemary on the grill by holding it with tongs over high heat until the leaves start to smoke (you can also let it catch fire and blow it out after a couple seconds). Place 1 sprig in each of 4 rocks glasses filled with ice and put the remaining sprigs in a cocktail shaker. Add the gin, lemon juice, and simple syrup to the shaker with ice. Shake well and strain into the glasses. Garnish with lemon slices, if desired.

To make the perfect margarita, just think "2:1:1"—two parts tequila, one part lime, and one part sweetener (in my case, the orange liqueur Cointreau). This recipe adds smoky notes from grilled lime as well as the chipotle salt rim.

# Smoky 211 Margarita

*Makes 4*

Wipe the grill grates with oil to prevent sticking. Build a medium-heat fire. Your medium-heat zone should have embers 3 to 5 inches from the cooking surface.

Coat the cut side of the limes with honey and place, cut side down, over medium heat until charred and soft, about 4 minutes. Remove from heat and, when they are cool enough to handle, squeeze the lime halves to get ½ cup juice.

Mix salt and chipotle in a 2:1 ratio. Moisten rims of 4 glasses with the squeezed lime halves and dip into the chipotle salt. Fill glasses with ice.

Add the lime juice to a cocktail shaker with the tequila, Cointreau, and a couple ice cubes. Shake very well and strain into prepared glasses.

**5 limes, halved**

**Honey, for coating**

**Salt and ground chipotle chile**

**1 cup tequila**

**½ cup Cointreau**

Thyme goes beautifully with sweet and citrus flavors, making it perfect for cocktails. This recipe multiplies easily for large groups; just blend the thyme and lemon juice in a blender and strain before adding to the other ingredients.

# Thyme Out

Makes 8

Wipe the grill grates with oil to prevent sticking. Build a high-heat fire. Your high-heat zone should have embers 1 to 2 inches from the cooking surface, with occasional flames licking it.

Place the lemons, cut side down, over high heat until they are charred and soft, about 3 minutes. While the lemons char, using tongs, hold 8 of the thyme sprigs over high heat just until they start to color and give off wisps of smoke.

Add the remaining 8 thyme sprigs to a cocktail shaker, squeeze in the lemon juice, and add a couple ice cubes. Shake very well and strain into a pitcher. Add the ice water, vodka, and agave, and stir until the agave is dissolved.

Serve the drinks in ice-filled glasses garnished with a charred thyme sprig.

8 lemons, halved
16 sprigs of thyme
Ice cubes
4 cups ice water
1½ cups vodka
½ cup agave or simple syrup (see page 230)

# Bloody Mary

Makes 4

Keep this recipe in the back of your mind when you have the grill going on a Friday or Saturday night, for morning-after brunch drinks with fresh-grilled flavor. But even if you don't want Bloody Marys, it's a good mix to have in your fridge. Use it as a marinade for skirt steak, to spice up tomato or minestrone soup, whisked with olive oil for a salad dressing, or mixed with a little tomato sauce for grilled shrimp cocktail. (It's also delicious with beer instead of vodka: use 12 ounces of ice-cold beer per serving, and serve in pint glasses without ice.)

3 plum tomatoes, about 10 ounces total

½ habanero chile, stemmed and seeded (use gloves or a paper towel when handling habaneros)

½ garlic clove

1 tablespoon fresh or store-bought horseradish

1 tablespoon Worcestershire sauce

1 tablespoon freshly squeezed lemon juice

6 ounces vodka

Celery sticks, lemon wedges, and/or pickled peperoncini, for garnish

Wipe the grill grates with oil to prevent sticking. Build a medium-heat fire. Your medium-heat zone should have embers 3 to 5 inches from the cooking surface.

Grill the tomatoes over medium heat, turning occasionally, until lightly charred and soft all over, about 10 minutes. Meanwhile, using tongs, hold the habanero over medium heat until it starts to brown and soften, about 2 minutes. Transfer the tomatoes and habanero to a blender together with the garlic, horseradish, Worcestershire, and lemon juice. Blend until very smooth, then strain through a fine-mesh strainer or cheesecloth into a pitcher, discarding any tomato skins that remain. Stir in the vodka and divide among ice-filled glasses, garnishing as desired.

Note: Habanero chiles have fantastic fruity flavor but are extremely spicy. Most of the heat is in the seeds and the thin white veins; removing these will tame the heat considerably.

# About the Authors

Eric Werner is the chef and owner of Hartwood restaurant in Tulum, Mexico, which he opened with his wife, Mya Henry, in 2010. Situated between the Yucatán jungle and the Caribbean Sea, Hartwood is renowned for highlighting local Mayan ingredients and for its staunch dedication to wood-fire cooking. It has garnered acclaim from publications such as *Bon Appétit*, *Vogue*, and the *New York Times*. Werner originally embraced the primal, wood-fired cooking method in his formative years by cooking over campfires, and furthered his knowledge at a school for disenfranchised youth in New York's Catskill Mountains. After graduating from the Culinary Institute of America, he went on to work at Vinegar Hill House in Brooklyn and Peasant in NYC before moving with Mya to the Yucatán to construct his dream project: an environmentally sustainable outdoor restaurant serving vibrant and inspired seasonal food. Their first book, *Hartwood: Bright, Wild Flavors from the Edge of the Yucatán*, was released in 2015 and was the recipient of the IACP Cookbook Award for Culinary Travel.

Nils Bernstein was born and raised in Seattle and now splits his time between New York City, Mexico City, and the Mexican state of Yucatán. He traded a long career in the music industry, running the publicity departments for independent record labels Sub Pop and Matador, for one in food, drink, and travel writing. Bernstein is the food editor for *Wine Enthusiast* magazine, and he also writes and develops recipes for many other outlets. Eric's whole-kitchen home-grilling tips have permanently changed the way Bernstein cooks at home.

# Acknowledgments

**To the Hartwood kitchen**: this book would not have possible without your help and hard work. Thank you!

**To Amber Burling**: thank you very much for the great job you did with recipe development and recipe testing.

**To Francine Lee**: thank you very much for your dedication and efforts to *The Outdoor Kitchen*.

## Special thanks to:

Katherine Cowles

Mya Henry

Charlie Werner

Nils Bernstein

Andrea Gentl

Marty Hyers

Frankie Crichton

Piotr PM Welding

Emily Timberlake

Emma Rudolph

Emma Campion

Allison Renzulli

Jane Chinn

Mari Gill

Kristin Casemore

Dulci DeCarlo

Frank DeCarlo

Emily Isabella

Cheryl Rogowski

Andrea Gallego

Erick Celaya

Austin Simard

Jazmine Yurtin

Jon Santos

# Index

Published in the United States by Ten Speed Press,
an imprint of Random House, a division of
Penguin Random House LLC, New York.
www.tenspeed.com

Ten Speed Press and the Ten Speed Press colophon are
registered trademarks of Penguin Random House LLC.

Library of Congress Cataloging-in-Publication Data
Names: Werner, Eric, author. | Bernstein, Nils, 1968– author.
   | DeCarlo, Frank, writer of foreword. | Gentl & Hyers,
   photographer.
Title: The outdoor kitchen : live-fire cooking from Hartwood
   / Eric Werner with Nils Bernstein ; foreword by Frank
   DeCarlo ; photographs by Gentl and Hyers.
Description: Regular. | California : Ten Speed Press, 2020. |
   Includes bibliographical references and index. |
Identifiers: LCCN 2019031473 | ISBN 9780399582370
   (hardcover) | ISBN 9780399582387 (epub)
Subjects: LCSH: Outdoor cooking. | LCGFT: Cookbooks.
Classification: LCC TX823 .W453 2020 | DDC 641.5/78—dc23
LC record available at https://lccn.loc.gov/2019031473

Hardcover ISBN: 978-0-399-58237-0
eBook ISBN: 978-0-399-58238-7

Printed in China

Design by Emma Campion
Food styling by Andrea Gentl
Prop styling by Andrea Gentl and Mya Henry

10 9 8 7 6 5 4 3 2 1

First Edition